INCA

DISCOVER THE CULTURE AND GEOGRAPHY OF A LOST CIVILIZATION

WITH **25** PROJECTS

LAWRENCE KOVACS

Illustrated by Farah Rizvi

Dedication

For Krista, with love and admiration. Thank you for inviting me along on your amazing adventures. And to Isabel and Sophia, who have many more adventures ahead.

~ Latest Titles in the *Build It Yourself* Series ~

Check out more titles at www.nomadpress.net

green press
INITIATIVE

Nomad Press is committed to preserving ancient forests and natural resources. We elected to print *Inca: Discover the Culture and Geography of a Lost Civilization* on 4,507 lbs. of Williamsburg Recycled 30 percent offset.

Nomad Press made this paper choice because our printer, Sheridan Books, is a member of Green Press Initiative, a nonprofit program dedicated to supporting authors, publishers, and suppliers in their efforts to reduce their use of fiber obtained from endangered forests. For more information, visit **www.greenpressinitiative.org**

Nomad Press
A division of Nomad Communications
10 9 8 7 6 5 4 3 2 1

This book was manufactured by Sheridan Books,
Ann Arbor, MI USA.
March 2013 Job # 345118
ISBN: 978-1-61930-140-5

Illustrations by Farah Rizvi
Educational Consultant Marla Conn

Questions regarding the ordering of this book should be addressed to
Independent Publishers Group
814 N. Franklin St., Chicago, IL 60610
www.ipgbook.com

Nomad Press
2456 Christian St.
White River Junction, VT 05001
www.nomadpress.net

CONTENTS

Timeline of the Inca Civilization

c. 1000 CE

As the Tiahuanaco civilization disappears, the Andean highlands become occupied by hundreds of independent societies who often fight with each other. One of these groups, the Inca, takes up residence near the valley of Cuzco, Peru.

c. 1200 CE

The Inca eventually subdue the other groups in the Cuzco valley. It becomes a peaceful area compared to the regions filled with warring groups elsewhere in the Andes. The Inca live here in relative harmony and begin to create systems of civic organization and resource management.

1400–1438

As the eighth Inca ruler, Wiraqocha Inca, nears the end of his reign, Cuzco is taken over by the powerful Chanka army, a rival group. The Inca defeat the Chanka, which inspires the Inca to begin their expansion across western South America.

1438–1463

In 1438, an Inca prince who takes the name of Pachacuti ("Transformer of the Earth") becomes the Inca ruler, or Sapa Inca. Pachacuti lives up to his name, organizing enormous construction projects in and around the city of Cuzco. The Cuzco valley is literally transformed by enormous buildings made of fine stonework, hillsides covered in farming terraces, and rivers whose courses are altered.

1463–1493

Pachacuti's son, Thupa Inca Yupanki, leads an Inca army to defeat the Chimu Empire on the northern coast of Peru. In 1471, Thupa Inca Yupanki succeeds his father as the Sapa Inca. During his reign, the Inca Empire continues to expand, establishing a second Inca capital in Ecuador.

1493–1525

In 1493, Thupa Inca Yupanki dies, and his son, Wayna Qhapaq, becomes Sapa Inca. Under Wayna Qhapaq, massive construction projects continue, and the system of Inca roads grows. In 1525, Wayna Qhapaq dies during an outbreak of smallpox, a European disease. Smallpox was brought to the New World by Spanish explorers. By most estimates, the smallpox epidemic kills more than half of the native population.

1525–1532

After Wayna Qhapaq's death, two of his sons, Atahualpa and Huascar, fight for control of the Inca Empire. This civil war comes to an end when Atahualpa's army defeats Huascar's troops in Cuzco.

1532–1533

Francisco Pizarro, a Spanish explorer, sails from Panama with 160 men and around 60 horses. The Spaniards ambush Atahualpa in Cajamarca and take him hostage.

1533–1536

The Spanish murder Atahualpa and take over the city of Cuzco. They crown Manco Inca, a descendant of Wayna Qhapaq, the new ruler of the Inca, but his title is purely ceremonial. The Spanish take control of the empire.

1536–1538

After being double crossed many times by the Spanish, Manco Inca double crosses them himself and leads a year-long rebellion, burning Cuzco to the ground. During the siege, the Spaniards Diego de Almagro and Hernando Pizarro turn on each other and gather Inca armies to fight against each other on their behalf. Hernando Pizarro kills Almagro in 1538, and Francisco Pizarro's position as leader of Peru is secured.

1537–1572

Francisco Pizarro relocates to Lima where he is murdered by followers of Almagro in 1541. The Spanish continue to solidify their hold on Peru and launch an attack on the last Inca stronghold, Vilcabamba. The final Sapa Inca, Tupac Amaru, is captured and publicly killed in the center of Cuzco.

1780

Tupac Amaru II, a distant descendant of the Inca, mounts a rebellion against the Spanish. He is caught and executed spectacularly by the Spanish, along with his entire family.

1911

Hiram Bingham, a geography professor from Yale, discovers the lost city of Machu Picchu.

2011

Yale University returns 40,000 Machu Picchu artifacts to Peru. With permission from the government of Peru, these items were removed by Hiram Bingham in the early 1900s so that he could study them.

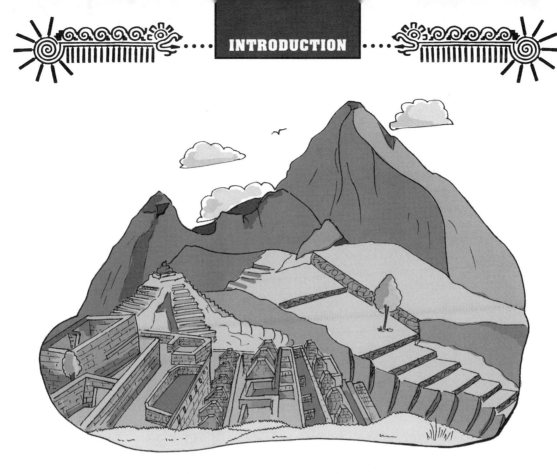

☀ Machu Picchu

Maybe you've heard of the lost city of Machu Picchu. It's one of the Seven Wonders of the World, visited by millions of people every year. This stunning ancient city made of stone blocks has been featured in museum exhibits, movies, books, paintings, and television shows.

You may know that Machu Picchu is located in the South American country of Peru and is built on a mountain. You may know that llamas and condors live there. But what do you know about the people who built it? Who were these talented craftspeople? How and why did they build this city where they did, and what were their beliefs?

The people who built Machu Picchu, and other sites like it, were called the Inca. Like many ancient **cultures**, the Inca started out small. But what's extraordinary about this **civilization** is how quickly it came to dominate the region and then how suddenly it was defeated. According to many **scholars**, the Inca Empire grew from an **isolated** group of farmers to the **New World's** most commanding power by around 1400 **CE**—only to crumble spectacularly by the mid 1500s.

Fortunately, much of what the Inca created during their short time in power was built to last. They used materials like granite, pottery, and gold. Also, the area where the Inca chose to build much of their **empire** is difficult to get to, high in the remote mountains of South America. This has allowed **archaeologists** to examine relatively undisturbed **relics** and ruins to come up with ideas about how the Inca lived.

WORDS TO KNOW

culture: a group of people and their beliefs and way of life.

civilization: a community of people that is advanced in art, science, and government.

scholar: someone who has done advanced study of a subject.

isolated: to be separate and apart from others.

New World: North and South America.

CE: put after a date, CE stands for Common Era. It counts up from zero to the present year.

empire: a group of countries, states, or lands that are ruled by one ruler.

archaeologist: a scientist who studies people through the objects they left behind.

relic: an object that is important because of its age or connection with the past.

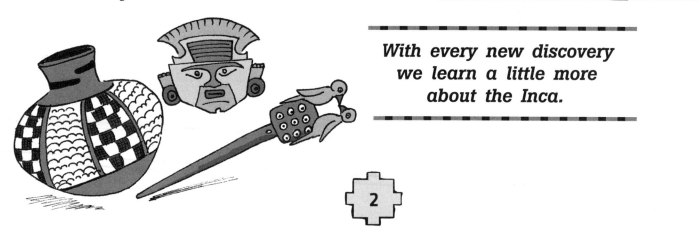

With every new discovery we learn a little more about the Inca.

But it's not an easy job. Because the Inca had no written language, they left behind no documents or texts describing their culture. So while scholars and explorers continue to make new discoveries about the Inca, much of their world remains a mystery.

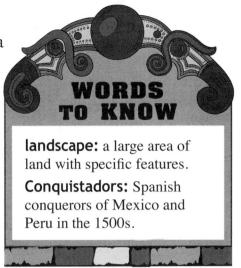

WORDS TO KNOW

landscape: a large area of land with specific features.

Conquistadors: Spanish conquerors of Mexico and Peru in the 1500s.

This book will help you understand what it might have been like to live as an Inca. You will learn about the unique **landscape** of South America, the religious beliefs of the Inca, their festivals, food, clothing, political power, and how they were defeated by the Spanish **Conquistadors**.

Almost all of the activities and projects in this book can be done with little adult supervision and materials that you already have in your house. So prepare to travel back in time to a place where people lived in harmony with nature, the heavens, and the mythical spirit world. Get ready to Build It Yourself.

◉ The Land of the Inca

The Inca traveled all over western South America and its wildly varied landscapes. There would have been many excellent locations to build a civilization on the South American continent. They chose to build the headquarters of Tawantinsuyu, the **Quechua** (ketch-oo-ah) name of their empire, in a remote and rugged mountain valley. It is in the center of the country now known as Peru. The name of the city they built, much of it still intact today, is **Cuzco**.

The city of Cuzco is very high up in the mountains. Its location at an **altitude** of 11,500 feet (3,500 meters) in the middle of the Cordillera Real (Cord-ee-yair-ah Ray-ahl) section of the **Andes Mountains** seems like a curious place to choose. At such high altitude, the **weather** in Cuzco can be extreme. Even today it is a difficult place to travel to or venture from. The Andes is a confusing and complicated collection of **peaks**, **valleys**, **ridges**, lakes, **escarpments**, rivers, **glaciers**, **plateaus**, and **canyons**. Also, the **Andean** region is prone to natural disasters like earthquakes, floods, and landslides.

So why would a civilization ever choose such a challenging place for its capital? There are three good reasons: the **climate**, the stars, and protection from enemies.

WORDS TO KNOW

Quechua: the language of the Inca, created to communicate with hundreds of different groups of people.

Cuzco: the Peruvian city that was the headquarters of the Inca Empire.

altitude: the height above the level of the sea. Also called elevation.

Andes Mountains: the mountain range that runs the length of western South America. It is the world's longest mountain range above sea level.

weather: temperature, cloudiness, rainfall, and wind.

peak: the pointed top of a mountain.

valley: a long, low area between hills or mountains, often following a river or stream.

ridge: a long, narrow high area of land, usually linking together mountains or hills.

escarpment: a long cliff, often as part of a ridge.

glacier: a large river of ice that moves down a mountain slope.

plateau: a large, raised area of land that is fairly flat and often cut by deep canyons.

canyon: a deep, narrow valley with steep sides.

Andean: relating to the Andes Mountains.

climate: average weather patterns in an area over many years.

Plate Tectonics

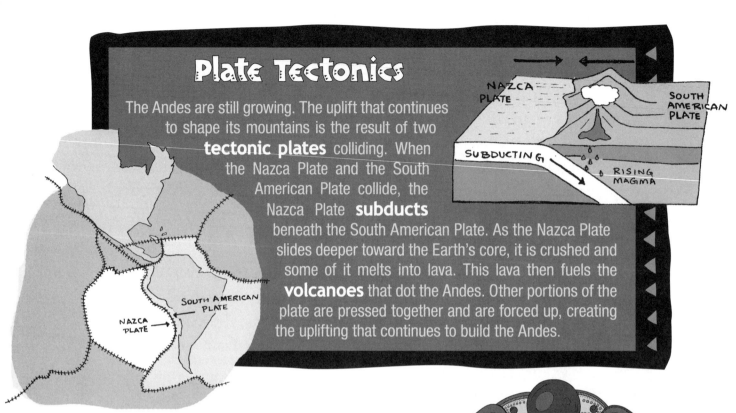

The Andes are still growing. The uplift that continues to shape its mountains is the result of two **tectonic plates** colliding. When the Nazca Plate and the South American Plate collide, the Nazca Plate **subducts** beneath the South American Plate. As the Nazca Plate slides deeper toward the Earth's core, it is crushed and some of it melts into lava. This lava then fuels the **volcanoes** that dot the Andes. Other portions of the plate are pressed together and are forced up, creating the uplifting that continues to build the Andes.

The Climate

The Inca, who were deeply connected to the natural world, became experts in how to thrive on some of the tallest mountains on the planet. And believe it or not, this had a lot to do with how this ancient culture became so successful, advanced, and powerful. It was hard for anyone to **conquer** the Inca because they lived in such a remote, difficult **environment**.

WORDS TO KNOW

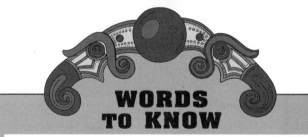

tectonic plate: a large slab of the earth's crust that is in constant motion. It moves on the hot, melted layer of earth below.

subduction: when one tectonic plate slides beneath another.

volcano: an opening in the earth's surface through which melted rock, ash, and gases erupt.

conquer: to defeat someone or something.

environment: everything in nature, living and nonliving, including animals, plants, rocks, soil, and water.

The weather and climate of any location is affected by many factors, but one thing that can make a big difference is the shape of the land. Because of the location and massive size of the Andes, the home base of the Inca does not have all four seasons of winter, spring, summer, and fall. There is just a rainy season and a dry season.

Over the Pacific Ocean, air travels from the west to the east. As this air passes over South America though, it is blocked and redirected north by the Andes. Meanwhile, on the east side of the continent, moist air from the Amazon is drawn west. This air, **saturated** with **water vapor**, is pushed high into the **atmosphere** by the steep slopes of the mountains.

WORDS TO KNOW

saturated: to be full of water.

water vapor: water as a gas, like steam or mist.

atmosphere: the gases that surround the earth.

condense: when water or another liquid cools down and changes from a gas (water vapor) back into a liquid (water).

precipitation: falling moisture in the form of rain, sleet, snow, or hail.

The higher the air rises, the colder it becomes. And the colder the air is, the less vapor it can hold. So the air releases moisture. It first **condenses**, turning into clouds, and then changes back into liquid water that falls from the sky in the form of **precipitation**.

PRECIPITATION

MOIST AIR

PACIFIC OCEAN

WORDS TO KNOW

katabatic wind: a high-speed wind that races down a mountain slope.

equator: an imaginary line around the earth, halfway between the North and South Poles.

crops: plants grown for food and other uses.

preserve: to save food in a way that it won't spoil.

This is why most very tall mountains that you see are covered in snow.

So the Inca were sometimes wet. But they also faced cold, dry **katabatic winds**. The Inca figured out how to use these winds to their advantage to dry grain and other food.

During sunny days, the hot sun near the **equator** heats the ground and the air around it. The warmed air rises up out of low valleys toward the peaks and glaciers of the Andes. As the sun begins to set, all that warm air that has risen is cooled, and flows back down to lower elevations, rushing like an invisible river down into the valleys and canyons. In places like Ollantaytambo, these winds happen every single day of the dry season. The Inca harnessed the winds to dry out their **crops** so they could be **preserved**.

COLD AIR

WARM AIR

SNOW SURFACE

The Stars

In the Andes region, the peaks soar to over 20,000 feet (6,100 meters). The air is so thin and clear that the stars and the planets look different in the sky than from almost anywhere else. Because of its amazing clarity, the night sky and **astronomy** were extremely important in Inca culture.

The Inca worshipped the sun (Inti) and the moon (Mama-Quilla) as gods. They looked to the stars for knowledge about the weather and when to plant crops. Prayers to the sun asked him to rise in the proper place for planting.

WORDS TO KNOW

astronomy: the movement of the sun, moon, and stars.

astronomical event: something that happens because of the movement of the sun, moon, or stars.

solstice: the day around June 21 and December 21 when the day is either shortest or longest depending on whether you are north or south of the equator.

constellation: a group of stars that form a shape.

The Inca built many of their temples so that during an **astronomical event** *like a* **solstice**, *shadows were cast on temple walls in the shapes of animals or mountain ranges.*

Like our Big Dipper, the Inca had their own **constellations**. Unlike us, however, they didn't "connect the dots" to create their shapes because there were too many stars! The sky was so clear where they lived, and the stars so bright and plentiful, that they found many constellations in the black spaces between the bright clusters of stars. The Inca looked to these "dark cloud" constellations, such as a partridge-like bird called Yutu, a celestial toad, and the Sky Llama, to mark important events and the passage of the seasons.

Did You Know?

The Inca watched for the rising of the Pleiades star cluster to signal the start of their year. We call the Pleiades the Seven Sisters after the seven brightest stars in the cluster, but the Inca could actually see 13 stars because of their clear air and high altitude.

Protection from Enemies

If you wanted to find a place where you would be safe from attacks by enemies, it would be hard to find a better spot than on the top of a mountain ridge. Ridges gave the Inca a wide open view of their surroundings and acted like a natural wall. Enemies were forced to scale cliffs to reach them.

But living on a ridge also comes with many challenges.

Most important, how would the Inca get water and food? In the settlements of Pisaq, Machu Picchu, Ollantaytambo, and Choquequirao, the Inca chose ridges that had natural springs at their crest.

This fresh, cold, clear water bubbling out of the ground was the most important factor that made it possible for the Inca to survive on top of mountain ridges. It must have taken them many years to locate such special places.

The Inca overcame their other challenge by developing **terraces** for growing crops. These terraces were often built on shockingly steep cliffs and looked to be suspended in the air. Some of the water from the spring was used to **irrigate** the crops in these terraces. So the Inca figured out how to protect themselves against enemy attack and feed themselves in the high Andes Mountains.

WORDS TO KNOW

terrace: an area of flat land carved into a hillside, often used for farming.

irrigate: to supply land with water, usually for crops.

Did You Know?

The Andes is the longest mountain range above water in the world. It runs for 4,300 miles (7,000 kilometers) like a spine down the length of South America, from the equator almost to Antarctica.

But the longest mountain range on the planet is actually under water. It's called the Mid-Ocean Ridge and spans the floor of five different oceans.

Màras and Moray

In the settlements of Màras and Moray near Cuzco, there are two sites that highlight the technological advances of the Inca. At Màras there is a vast network of hundreds of intricately terraced bright white salt pans tucked into a narrow valley above the Urubamba River. Each salt pool is about 250 square feet (76 square meters). An unusual spring there flows with salt water, and the terraces were designed by the Inca to **evaporate** the water, leaving pure salt behind. Salt is a vital **commodity** and was used in cooking and medicine. These terraces have been passed down to **descendants** of the Inca for over 600 years and are still in use today. They produce hundreds of pounds of salt every month.

At Moray, archaeologists discovered a series of circular terraces carved into low areas in the land. These are thought to have been agricultural "laboratories" for the Inca to develop and test different plants. There is a temperature difference of about 27 degrees Fahrenheit (15 degrees Celsius) between the top level and the bottom level. Each of the 25 terrace levels represents a different **microclimate** so the Inca could study the impact of different climates on a wide variety of crops.

WORDS TO KNOW

evaporate: when a liquid changes into a gas, causing the original substance to dry out.

commodity: an important raw material or agricultural product that can be bought or sold, like copper or coffee.

descendant: a person related to someone who lived in the past.

microclimate: the climate of a very small area.

MAKE YOUR OWN
ANDES LANDSCAPE

Most modern-day Peruvians describe their mountainous landscape as Papel Arrugado, which means, "crumpled paper." This activity will show you why.

Take a fresh piece of copier paper and crumple it up into a tight ball. Now, gently un-crumple it so that it still has ridges, imprints, and lines in it. Do not smooth out the paper. What you have created is a miniature model of a mountain range, and an example of what the Andes might look like from above.

If you could shrink yourself down to the size of a flea, what would it be like getting around this landscape? Can you imagine how difficult it would be to build trails and roads here? The Inca were able to do it, and they did it so well that many of the roads they built are still in place more than 500 years later!

MAKE YOUR OWN
CLOUD FOREST TERRARIUM

The Andean cloud forest is found on the eastern slope of the Andes Mountains. The warm, **humid** air from the **Amazon basin** makes its way up the mountains where it is blocked by cold, **denser** air there. The trapped air drops its moisture in the form of clouds and mist, quenching the thirst of the plants that grow in this unique **ecosystem**. A terrarium made from a soda bottle works like the cloud forest. The moist air near the **soil** rises up and is blocked by the top of the bottle where it condenses, creating ideal growing conditions for moisture-loving plants.

Hint: Ask an adult for help cutting the bottle.

1 Remove the label from the bottle. Turn the coffee cup upside down and then rest the marker on top of it. Hold the bottle upright with the marker resting against it about 6 inches up (15 centimeters). Rotate the bottle to draw a straight line all the way around it.

2 Cut the bottle along the line with a pair of scissors. You may need to start a small hole in the bottle before you can cut it with the scissors. Please ask a parent or adult to help you with the cutting.

3 Place a handful of stones in the bottom half of the bottle, about 1–2 inches deep (2½ to 5 centimeters).

4 Place the charcoal and then the soil in the bottle. Fill it to about 1 inch from the top of the cutoff section of the bottle (2½ centimeters).

SUPPLIES

- 2-liter soda bottle with cap
- coffee cup
- marker
- scissors
- handful of small stones or pebbles
- handful of activated charcoal
- 2 cups of potting soil (500 milliliters)
- seeds or seedlings (ferns, thyme, and oregano work well)
- water

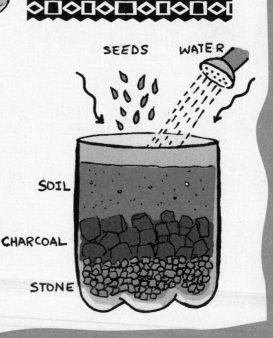

SEEDS   WATER

SOIL

CHARCOAL

STONE

WORDS TO KNOW

humid: when the air has a lot of moisture in it.

Amazon basin: the land area in central and eastern South America that the water flows across or under to reach the Amazon River.

dense: when something is tightly packed in its space.

ecosystem: a community of living and nonliving things and their environment. Living things are plants, animals, and insects. Nonliving things are soil, rocks, and water.

soil: the top layer of the earth.

7 Squeeze the top piece of the bottle onto the bottom half so the top is on the outside. If you have trouble fitting the two pieces together, cut a slit partway up the top half of the bottle.

8 Once the plants have sprouted you should make sure the bottle gets some sunlight, but not too much sunlight. Don't leave it in direct light for the entire day. It is a closed environment and can get very hot inside.

9 Look carefully at the soil in the terrarium. It should look moist but not soaked or too dry. Beads of water should form on the inside of the top of the bottle. Moisture should drip down the sides and continue to water the soil. If it appears to be too wet you can always take the top off and leave it uncovered for a day or two.

5 Plant your seeds or seedlings. You should plant six to ten seeds. Later, as they grow, you can pluck out some of the weaker ones and leave the two or three best ones.

6 Water your terrarium before placing the top on it. The soil should be moist but not soaked.

NAVIGATE USING THE STARS

The Inca knew a great deal about the stars, the planets, and their cycles. Since their home territory was at such a high altitude, the stars were clearly visible. The Inca used their understanding of astronomy for ceremonies, marking the passage of time, and **agriculture**. This activity will teach you to use the stars in the **Northern Hemisphere**. In North America, because of light from streetlights and cities and the lower altitude, we can see fewer stars than the Inca could. But there is one constellation that is visible to us all year long that can be used for navigation. It is part of the constellation Ursa Major (the Big Bear) and is called the Big Dipper.

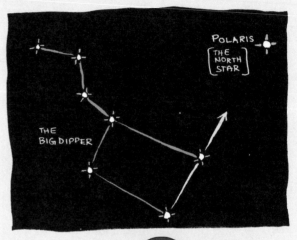

1 Choose a moonless night. If you don't know which way is north, this activity will help you find it.

2 About one-third of the way between the **horizon** and the top of the sky, find a group of seven stars that looks like a ladle. This is the Big Dipper. If you draw an imaginary line from the far edge of the ladle up into the sky, it will come close to intersecting a bright star. This star is Polaris, the North Star.

3 Polaris can be used to figure out the **cardinal directions** from your position. Wherever you are, this star points you north. When you are facing north, the sun will set to your left, in the west, and will rise to your right, in the east. Draw a bird's-eye view of your house, and using the Big Dipper and Polaris, map out the cardinal directions from your home.

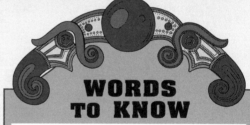

WORDS TO KNOW

agriculture: growing crops and raising animals for food.

Northern Hemisphere: the half of the earth north of the equator.

horizon: the point in the distance where the sky and the earth (or the sea) seem to meet.

cardinal directions: the main points on a compass—north, south, east, and west.

CHAPTER 2

☀ Conquest of a Continent

At the height of their power, no other civilization in the history of the world had control of as much land as the Inca. How were they able to create such a vast and powerful empire? They used their skills as **politicians**, **engineers**, warriors, and **bureaucrats**.

WORDS TO KNOW

politician: someone who is part of the government.

engineer: someone who designs or builds roads, bridges, and buildings.

bureaucrat: someone who helps run a government.

WORDS TO KNOW

pre-Columbian: the time before Christopher Columbus came to the New World.

predecessors: people who came before.

artifact: an object made by people in the past, including tools, pottery, and jewelry.

adapt: to change to survive in new or different conditions.

diverse: many different people or things.

Until recently, the Inca were thought of as a tribe of mighty warriors who conquered much of western South America in an amazingly short amount of time. What we now know paints a slightly different picture. Yes, the Inca were an advanced civilization that quickly dominated the people around them, but they were not the first organized civilization in **pre-Columbian** South America. We just know more about the Inca than their **predecessors** because the Inca were the civilization in power when the Europeans arrived.

Archaeologists have discovered and studied **artifacts** *from many other advanced civilizations that came before the Inca.*

What happened to those other civilizations? What was it about the Inca that allowed them to completely dominate and defeat their competitors? The Inca figured out how to **adapt** to a world that was physically changing, and they learned how to control the **diverse** groups of people they conquered.

Conquering the Climate

Our planet is a constantly changing place. Even when a civilization carefully chooses where to build its empire, the physical **characteristics** of that place can change. And change can happen quickly. A volcano erupting or an earthquake rattling can alter the landscape quickly. But change can also happen slowly, such as when weather patterns or soil composition change over time. Some changes can happen so slowly that people don't even realize they are happening at all.

In the years before the rise of the Inca, a slow change began in the **foothills** of the Andes. The **stable** weather patterns and **fertile** soil conditions began to disappear. Rising temperatures and **drought** affected the growing conditions that the farmers and herders had depended on for hundreds of years. This **climate change** is probably what toppled the Huari civilization around 1100 CE.

WORDS TO KNOW

characteristic: a feature of a person, place, or thing.

foothill: a low hill at the base of a mountain.

stable: regular and predictable.

fertile: land that is good for growing plants.

drought: a long period of time without rain.

climate change: a change in the long term average weather patterns of a place.

The Huari were powerful predecessors of the Inca who dominated the Andes beginning around 550 CE. The collapse of the Huari left the people of the high Andean region without an organized government, on top of shortages of food and water.

What happened next? Local Andean chiefs became more powerful and raided neighboring villages for whatever food they could find. Many of the inhabitants of these villages fled to the **barren** lands above 13,000 feet (4,000 meters), to the bitterly cold, windy **puna**. But in the Cuzco valley, a **formidable** group of farmers known as the Inca fought these chiefs off. Instead of **retreating** like other communities, the Inca farmers joined together to defend their lands.

WORDS TO KNOW

barren: bare land with poor soil and few plants.

puna: a high, flat area in the Andes.

formidable: large, powerful, and difficult to defeat.

retreat: to withdraw from something threatening.

Did You Know?

Scientists are able to learn about historical weather patterns by looking at the ice in a glacier. Some glaciers in the Peruvian Andes are tens of thousands of years old, and every year, a new layer of snow is deposited on them. By drilling a deep core sample of the glacial ice and examining each layer, scientists can uncover patterns of drought, flood, temperature change, and even forest fires and volcanic eruptions.

Cuzco, like most other locations where the Inca chose to settle, has excellent agricultural **resources**. The city is located inside a huge **alpine cirque** with rivers emptying into it from the highlands above. The growing fields are located in high, cool elevations above the city.

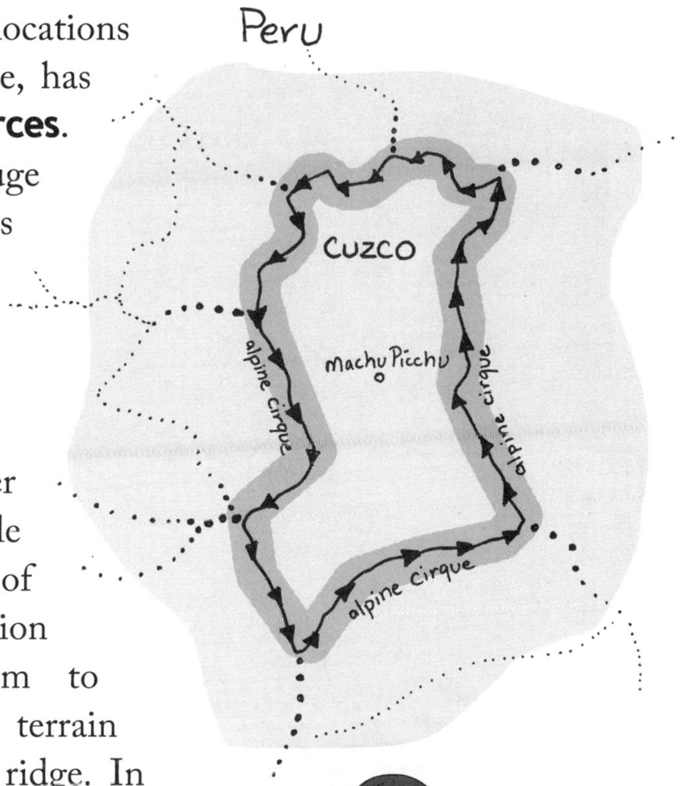

Because they were clever engineers, the Inca were able to build enormous systems of terraces and intricate irrigation channels. This allowed them to **cultivate** the higher, steeper terrain near the crest of the Cuzco ridge. In fact, their agricultural advances allowed the Inca to grow more crops than they could eat in a season, so they learned to preserve and store their food. Some archaeologists believe that this surplus food allowed surplus **labor** to be used for other purposes.

Some men could give up farming and fight as soldiers in the Inca army.

Peru

Cuzco

alpine cirque

Machu Picchu

alpine cirque

alpine cirque

WORDS TO KNOW

resources: something used by people to help them take care of themselves.

alpine cirque: a bowl-shaped mountain valley.

cultivate: to use land for farming.

labor: work, or people who do work.

21

Lake Titicaca: The Decisive Battleground

High on the **altiplano** between the countries of Peru and Bolivia sits Lake Titicaca, the world's highest **navigable** lake. The lake, with its vast stores of fresh water, sits at an elevation of 12,500 feet (3,800 meters). The surrounding area provides an ideal place for llamas and alpacas to graze. The mountains surrounding the lake are rich with precious metals like gold and silver. In the mid-1400s, the Inca king named Pachacuti took an enormous chance invading the Titicaca area, but the risk paid off. By defeating the various Titicaca lords, the Inca took control of one of the most important regions for their success.

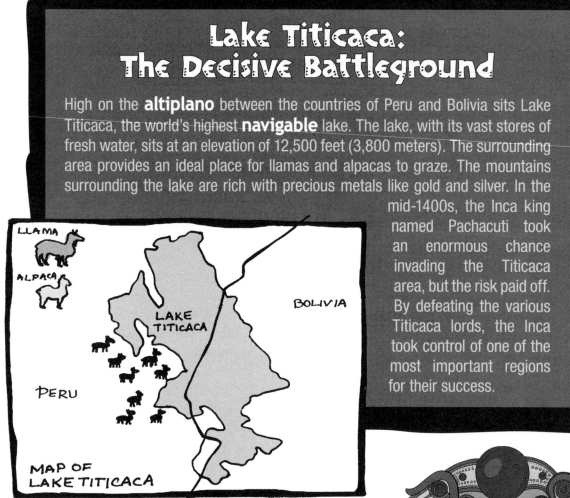

MAP OF LAKE TITICACA

How to Manage an Empire

The accomplishments of the Inca were monumental and innovative. But most Andean scholars would probably agree that the Inca's true genius was in controlling the people they conquered. There were three elements to their strategy.

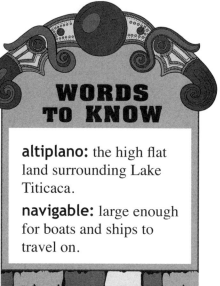

WORDS TO KNOW

altiplano: the high flat land surrounding Lake Titicaca.

navigable: large enough for boats and ships to travel on.

Centralization: The Inca **centralized** their power in the city of Cuzco, which the Inca believed was the center of the entire universe. Inca **royalty** lived in Cuzco, the holiest Inca temples were built there, and both the government and the military were based there. This centralization of power and resources gave the Inca an edge over their rivals, whose civilizations were not as large or organized.

Language: The Inca required everyone in their empire to learn and use their Quechua language for official state business. The Inca called the language *runasimi*, which means "human speech." The Spanish reported that there were three principal languages in use at the time of their contact with the Inca: Quechua, Aymara, and Puquina. Hundreds of other languages disappeared as cultures were absorbed by the Inca and then conquered by the Spanish.

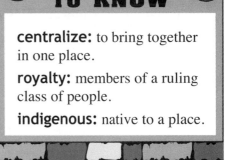

Did You Know?

In the highland regions of modern-day South America, much of the **indigenous** population still speaks either Quechua or Aymara.

WORDS TO KNOW

centralize: to bring together in one place.

royalty: members of a ruling class of people.

indigenous: native to a place.

Administration: The Inca created a complex system of rules and practices to manage their growing empire. With this **administration** they were able to control an estimated 6 to 9 million people living over an area of 386,000 square miles (1 million square kilometers). Because the Inca didn't use money, their economy was based on the value of labor.

Subjects of the Inca Empire were required to pay **tribute** to the state. They donated a portion of their crops, labor, **textiles**, or other items of value each year to Inca rulers. Some of the tribute collected was set aside for storage, and warehouses of food, textiles, and weapons were created.

WORDS TO KNOW

administration: a system to manage a large group of people, such as a city or country.

tribute: a gift or act intended to show respect, gratitude, or admiration.

textiles: cloth or fabric.

The food storehouses served two purposes. In case of a bad harvest, people could survive on the food that had been preserved and stored. This gave them some incentive to pay. The Inca also needed a way to get meals and weapons to their soldiers who traveled far and wide to expand the empire. The storehouses served as remote **caches** that the military could use while out on their missions.

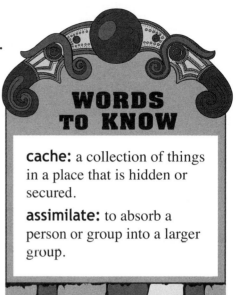

WORDS TO KNOW

cache: a collection of things in a place that is hidden or secured.

assimilate: to absorb a person or group into a larger group.

The Inca kept records of their people and supplies, and who paid what tribute and when. Even without an alphabetical system of writing, they kept records on *quipus* (kee-pooz). These were multicolored threads hung like pendants from a central string. The threads had knots tied in them to signify numbers.

Using quipus, the Inca kept close track of the number of people living in an area, the types and number of weapons in storage buildings, and the surplus food stored in warehouses.

The Inca recognized that the people they conquered had their own beliefs and religions. Instead of forcing them to forget their beliefs, the Inca tried to win them over by allowing them to bring their gods into the Inca religion. In this way, the Inca **assimilated** new communities into their growing empire.

25

Not everyone was happy to be part of the big Inca plan. But when people chose not to cooperate with the Inca takeover of a community, they were removed from their villages. Loyal Incas from Cuzco were then sent to the village. This sent a clear message to everyone that resistance to the Inca was pointless.

The Keshwa Chaca of Huinchiri

Near the town of Huinchiri, north of Cuzco, the last remaining Inca Rope Bridge spans a canyon above the rushing waters of the Apurímac River. This bridge is made of cables braided from *qqoya* (koy-ah), a type of grass that grows in the Andean highlands. The Keshwa Chaca (Quechua Bridge) is rebuilt every year in June by local community members, since the *qqoya* straw breaks down as it weathers. Bridges like this one were probably used throughout the Inca Empire, but this is the last one in existence. It's likely that the labor to reconstruct the bridge each year was a tax levied by the Inca on the local population.

Roads

As the Inca began eyeing new areas to take over, they improved the pathways and trade routes that were already there and added to them. What they created was an astonishing highway complete with the ancient equivalent of rest stops, hotels, and restaurants. It linked together around 25,000 miles of paved roadway (40,000 kilometers).

The roads were not paved with asphalt the way our modern roads are, but with a patchwork of cobblestones, dirt, sand, and grass. In difficult areas they built steps, tunnels, and even suspension bridges.

The Inca roads were only open to people on official business. These were members of the Inca royalty, the military, and Inca messengers called *chaski*. The *chaski* had messenger stations called *chaskiwasi* about every 5 miles (8 kilometers), so each messenger would only have to run a short distance to make a delivery.

It is believed that in addition to delivering spoken messages, the *chaski* also carried knotted *quipus*. Using *quipus* was a way to make sure messages didn't get completely changed after being passed between so many people. It wasn't a game of telephone they were playing! The *chaski* system may have been so efficient that messengers could cover around 200 miles per day (322 kilometers). So fresh seafood could get from the coast to a ruler in the mountains without it going bad!

Did You Know?

The *chaskis* blew an alert from a conch shell called a *pututu* to alert the next messenger they were coming. The conch shell came from the Pacific coast and had a mouthpiece made from pine tar, similar in shape to what you might see on a trumpet.

MAKE YOUR OWN
QUIPU

European explorers were amazed that the Inca did not have a written language. It appeared that all cultural information was passed down orally from one generation to the next. But as it turns out the Inca did have a system for recording information, called the *quipu*. The *quipu* was a set of knotted strings that scholars now believe represented numbers and maybe even the syllables of words. Considering their advanced understanding of astronomy, agriculture, architecture, and government, it is remarkable that the Inca recorded their history through the *quipu*.

1 Attach one of each of the colored threads to the larger, braided yarn by tying a knot.

2 Tie knots in the colored strings. A single knot stands for the number one. A knot with two loops stands for two, and a knot with three loops stands for three, etc.

3 It is believed that *quipus* were read from left to right, like English words. You can try to create a message in your *quipu* by making the knots correspond to letters of the English alphabet. For example, one knot stands for the letter *a*, two knots stands for the letter *b*, and so on. If your message has the letter *z* in it you'll have to get pretty good at tying big knots! See if you can spell your name or even write a sentence with your *quipu*.

➤ SUPPLIES ◄

- 3 feet each (about 1 meter) of different colors of string, thread, or yarn (white, blue, yellow, red, black, green, and brown)
- white braided yarn, larger in diameter than the colored strings
- scissors

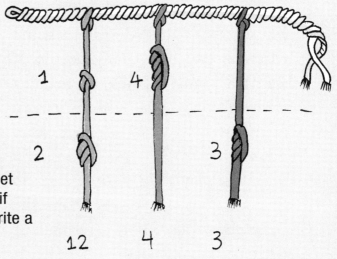

MAKE YOUR OWN
SOFT INCA BATTLE CLUB

The Inca had an organized military force with clear tactics and strategies. Since they were a civilization made up of a collection of the different cultures they conquered, the variety of weapons they used reflected this. One of the most common weapons used during Inca ground battles was the Inca mace. It was a wooden handle topped with a star-shaped head made of copper or stone.

Be Careful: Ask an adult for help using the hot glue gun.

1 Remove the center tube from a roll of paper towels.

2 Draw a six-sided, **symmetrical** star shape on the sheet of oak tag and cut it out. The **diameter** of the star should be around three times bigger than the diameter of the paper towel tube.

3 Use the oak tag star as a template, and trace its shape onto three pieces of corrugated cardboard. Cut out the cardboard stars.

4 Stack the three cardboard stars on top of each other. Have an adult help you use the hot glue gun to glue them in place to make one thicker star and glue the star to the end of the paper towel tube.

5 Cover the star and handle in aluminum foil. You can draw on the aluminum foil with the brown marker to make it look like copper.

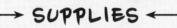

SUPPLIES

- tube from the center of a paper towel roll
- oak tag or other stiff paper
- scissors
- corrugated cardboard
- hot glue gun
- aluminum foil
- brown marker

WORDS TO KNOW

symmetrical: the same on all sides.

diameter: the line through the center of a circle, from one side to the other.

BUILD YOUR OWN
MINIATURE ROPE BRIDGE

The Inca used rope bridges made of woven grass to cross narrow river canyons. In this activity you will make a miniature version of the Keshwa Chaca (Quechua Bridge).

1 Imagine the walls of the box are the walls of a canyon, and the bottom of the box is the river. Color a river on the bottom of the box, and draw designs on the inside walls of the box to make them look like cliffs.

2 Use the pencil to make attachment points. Poke one hole near the top edge of each short side of the box, opposite each other. This will be the attachment for one of the handrails. Measure the distance from one hole to the other and cut a piece of string that is 5 inches longer (12½ centimeters).

→ SUPPLIES ←

- cardboard shoebox
- markers or crayons
- pencils
- scissors
- ruler
- braided string or twine (like packaging string or kite string)

3 To tie up one handrail, thread one end of the string through one hole, and tie it there with a double knot. Attach the other end of the string to the opposite side in the same way.

4 For the other handrail, move over 3 inches (7½ centimeters) and make two holes opposite each other like you did in step 2. These will be the attachments for the other handrail. Attach a string between these two holes.

5 Between each of the pairs of attachment holes, poke a hole that is 2 inches lower (5 centimeters). This will be the attachment for the bottom strand of the bridge.

6 Attach a string between the two bottom holes. Thread the string through the hole and then tie it around a pencil to hold it in place. Do the same on the other side.

7 Make the sides. Attach lengths of string to one handrail, wrap it around the bottom strand twice, then tie it to the opposite handrail. Repeat this process every inch or two all the way across the bridge (about every 5 centimeters). **Congratulations! You've made a miniature Keshwa Chaca!**

Llamas and Alpacas

The llama and alpaca are hoofed animals, related to the camel, that are native to South America. Llamas are the larger of the two and have been used for thousands of years as pack animals. They can carry up to 70 pounds (32 kilograms) and are a source of wool and food. Alpacas are smaller and their wool is softer and more lightweight, making it more desirable for clothing and textiles. Having herds of these animals gave the Inca an enormous advantage in their military campaigns. With alpacas and llamas they had food, wool, leather for clothing, and a way to carry their belongings.

MAKE UP YOUR OWN
"LANGUAGE"

The creation of a language takes a lot of time. It is a complex process that evolves over time. You can create a fun, made-up language by making a few changes to your own.

1 Add a one-syllable sound (that begins with a vowel) after each consonant in a word.

2 For the vowels in the word, just say their name (a, e, i, o, u).

3 For example, using the sound "in" in the word "hamburger" would sound like:

hin-a-min-bin-u-rin-gin-e-rin.

4 Practice your pretend language with a friend and see if you can carry on conversations without other people understanding what you are saying!

5 Come up with a fun name for your language.

GIN-OO-DIN TIN-O SIN-EE YIN-OU.

I-MIN HIN-A-PPIN-YIN TIN-O BIN-E HIN-E-RIN.

Did You Know?

If you visit the Andes region today, you'll find that there are more than 10 million speakers of variations of the Quechua language.

CHAPTER 3

☼ Religion

The Inca were a **spiritual** and **ceremonial** people. They believed in one creator of the universe, called Wiraqocha, the "creator of all things." Other, lesser gods were extensions of him. Most of these lesser **deities** were related to real aspects of the physical world, like the sun, moon, stars, **landforms**, and weather.

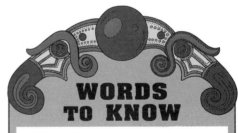

WORDS TO KNOW

spiritual: religious; relating to the soul or spirit.

ceremonial: using ceremonies to celebrate special events.

deity: a god or goddess.

landform: a physical feature of the earth's surface, such as a mountain or a valley.

Surprisingly, even though Wiraqocha was considered the original creator of the world, there were not many temples devoted to him.

WIRAQOCHA

INTI

Inti, the god of the sun, had a temple devoted to him in every Inca settlement. The Inca considered themselves the children of the sun and believed that gold was the sweat of the sun. The Temple of the Sun in Cuzco (K'oricancha) had at least one chamber whose walls were covered entirely in solid gold to reflect and celebrate the sun's light.

Illapa was the god of thunder, lightning, rainbows, and other elements of weather. The Inca imagined him as a warrior in the night sky with a sling in one hand and a club in the other. He was believed to create lightning by hurling stones from his sling and to bring rain by pouring down the stars of the **Milky Way**.

Mama-Quilla was the moon goddess and the wife of the sun. The Temple of the Moon in Cuzco was built to honor her. It is at the top of the ridge that surrounds the city and has many **altars**. The Inca believed that silver came from the tears of Mama-Quilla.

MAMA-QUILLA

WORDS TO KNOW

Milky Way: the faint band of light across the night sky made up of a cluster of vast numbers of stars in our galaxy.

altar: a raised area where religious ceremonies are performed.

Qollqa is the Quechua word for storehouse, and the name of the god of storehouses. This god was imagined to be the constellation called the Pleiades, which is a tight cluster of stars resembling a bundle of crops. It returns to the night sky of the **Southern Hemisphere** each year at harvest time.

Pachamama was the earth-mother goddess. Farmers made **sacrifices** to Pachamama for healthy and abundant harvests. Today, Peruvians still make offerings to her by spilling the first sip of their drink on the ground before drinking it themselves. Mamacocha was the god of the lakes and the sea. This god was most important to the people who lived along the coast.

PACHAMAMA

The Inca considered themselves to be people **descended** *from the sun and built elaborate* **shrines** *on mountaintops to get closer to the celestial bodies they worshipped.*

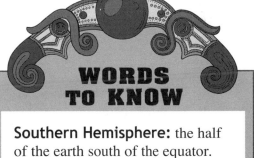

WORDS TO KNOW

Southern Hemisphere: the half of the earth south of the equator.

sacrifice: the killing of a person or animal as an offering to a god.

descended: to be related by birth.

shrine: a special, religious place.

mummy: a dead body that has been preserved so that it doesn't decay.

The Inca combined lavish ceremony with a deep understanding of the natural world and the universe. Women, children, and animals were sacrificed to the Gods. Dead kings were preserved as **mummies** and maintained all their power and property, even in death.

WORDS TO KNOW

monarchy: a form of government where all power is given to a single individual.

class levels: the ranks of people's status in society. The upper class has the most wealth and control, the middle class consists of skilled workers and managers, and the lower class works at the worst jobs for the lowest pay.

The simplest way to describe the organization of Inca culture is to call it a **monarchy**. One monarch, or king, was in charge. He inherited power from his father and passed it down to one of his sons after he died. But the empire was really a lot more complicated. There were different **class levels**, and the Inca believed that the world was full of people, both living and dead, as well as Gods and the spirits.

The Sapa Inca

Can you imagine a life where you were carried everywhere by servants and never stepped foot on the ground? Can you imagine wearing exquisite clothing that was only used once, and eating all your meals from dishes made of gold? This was the life of the ruler of the Inca Empire, the Sapa Inca (*Unique Inca* in Quechua).

The Sapa Inca ruled and owned everything. The first Sapa Inca was believed to be a child of Inti the Sun God.

The position of emperor was passed down to a son of the next generation. But if an emperor and his wife had more than one son, it wasn't always the oldest son who became the next Sapa Inca. It was the son chosen as more worthy.

WORDS TO KNOW

litter: a couch with poles used to carry a person.

The Sapa Inca was allowed to have as many wives as he wanted, but he had just one official wife, who was also his full sister.

Most of what we know about Inca royalty comes from stories written by the conquistadors. They captured and imprisoned the last Sapa Inca, Atahualpa. No one was allowed to look directly at the emperor because his image was considered too powerful for human eyes to handle. Before approaching him, visitors had to remove their footwear and carry something heavy. As they addressed the emperor, they kissed his hands and feet while he looked away.

Did You Know?

The emperor traveled on a beautiful **litter** carried by Rucanas. These were men chosen for their perfectly even walking gate. Walking ahead of the Rucanas, boys swept the ground to get rid of impurities before the emperor crossed it.

Everything the Sapa Inca touched—leftover food, clothing, dishes, blankets—was collected each day and saved to be burned at an annual festival. Even his fingernail clippings and strands of hair were saved. The emperor's clothing was all handwoven by *mamakuna* (momma-koo-nah), the most skillful female priestesses in the land, and was never worn twice.

WORDS TO KNOW

chicha: a beer made from corn.

The Mamakuna: Moon Priestesses

The *mamakuna* were a group of women who were married to the sun, similar to the way nuns are considered married to god. The *mamakuna* and their students were followers of the Inca god of the moon.

The *mamakuna* were forbidden to fall in love with men and lived together in a special school called the *aqllawasi* (ahk-yah-wah-see) with young girls called aqllas (ahk-yas). *Aqllas* were chosen for their beauty at the age of 10 from all corners of the Inca Empire and were highly respected in society. They were taught to spin wool, weave cloth, and prepare **chicha**.

After completing her training, an *aqlla* either became a *mamakuna* or was given permission by the Sapa Inca to marry a high-ranking member of the Inca elite. If a member of the *aqllawasi* broke the rules and fell in love with a man, it was considered a terrible crime. The woman, man, and the man's entire family were killed as well as all their animals. Their buildings were burned, and their fields were covered with salt so no crops could ever grow there again.

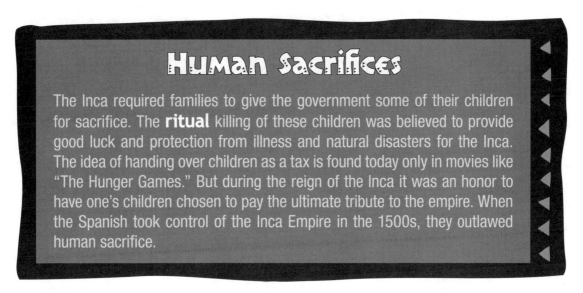

Human Sacrifices

The Inca required families to give the government some of their children for sacrifice. The **ritual** killing of these children was believed to provide good luck and protection from illness and natural disasters for the Inca. The idea of handing over children as a tax is found today only in movies like "The Hunger Games." But during the reign of the Inca it was an honor to have one's children chosen to pay the ultimate tribute to the empire. When the Spanish took control of the Inca Empire in the 1500s, they outlawed human sacrifice.

When a new Sapa Inca came to power, his **coronation** was a large celebration for the most important lords of the Inca Empire, and included many sacrifices. It is believed that children were killed along with large numbers of llamas. The children were buried with **ornamental** sculptures made of silver and gold to please Wiraqocha. The bodies of the llamas were burned.

Once a Sapa Inca, Always a Sapa Inca

After his death, the Sapa Inca entered the world of Uku Pacha. Mummified in a seated position, he was still treated as a king. His palace remained in his possession, as did his servants. **Dignitaries** "consulted" him for advice and he went on frequent trips to visit his relatives and country estates, carried on a litter by his Rucanas.

WORDS TO KNOW

ritual: something done as part of a religion.

coronation: the ceremony of crowning a new king.

ornamental: decorative.

dignitary: a person considered important because of high rank or office.

Mummies

Many cultures of South America practiced mummification of their dead kings. But since most of the tombs have been raided and robbed, we don't know for sure who else they chose to mummify.

One of the most amazing Inca mummies ever found was named Juanita by Dr. Johan Reinhard, the archaeologist who discovered her. She was a girl between 12 and 14 with intricately braided hair found at the summit of Mount Ampato in the Andes Mountains at an altitude of 20,630 feet (6,288 meters). Imagine how cold and difficult it must have been for the Inca to conduct a ceremony on top of this high peak without special mountain climbing equipment and clothing! Unlike other mummies who are dried out, Juanita was frozen solid. This has allowed scientists to examine her body—her muscles, her bones, and even the contents of her stomach.

Before beginning the climb to the summit of Mount Ampato to be sacrificed, the young girl ate a feast of vegetables. It appears the Inca did not want anyone to arrive in the spirit world hungry. She was probably exhausted and delirious by the time she arrived at the top. She remained kneeling there for more than 500 years, until Dr. Reinhard discovered her in 1996. Juanita now resides in a special refrigerated museum case in the city of Arequipa, Peru.

The ceremonies surrounding the death of the Sapa Inca may have been even more elaborate than those for the coronation of the new king. All the clothing that had been worn in the **mourning** ceremonies was burned along with a thousand adult llamas and a thousand newborn llamas. Two thousand more llamas were killed and eaten while other groups of llamas were burned in each of the places the Sapa Inca had visited in his lifetime.

WORDS TO KNOW

mourning: grieving after death.

> *When the Sapa Inca Pachacuti was preparing for his funeral, he insisted that boys and girls be brought and buried for him in the places where he slept and usually enjoyed himself.*

The Sacred Valley and the Milky Way

The Urubamba River valley descends from the base of the Cuzco valley and winds its way toward the jungles of the Amazon. It is often referred to as the Sacred Valley of the Inca. Within its steep walls are a series of ruins that are amazing for their beauty, their enormous size, and their excellent state of preservation. Many of the ruins here were originally built as elaborate retreats for the Inca royalty, but some served more practical purposes.

PERU

CUZCO • RIVER URUBAMBA

The Inca believed that the entire universe was living, and that each person on Earth had a common ancestor in the stars. They referred to the band of stars in the Milky Way as *mayu*, the Quechua word for river.

The Urubamba River was considered the earthly version of the heavenly "river" that could be seen in the night sky. According to Inca **mythology**, these two great rivers of the Inca universe came together at the edge of the sky where they both drew from the waters of an enormous ocean that surrounded the earth.

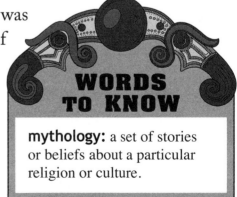

WORDS TO KNOW

mythology: a set of stories or beliefs about a particular religion or culture.

Did You Know?

The Inca had a sculpture known as Punchao (poon-chow), which was an image of the sun itself. From its special room in the Temple of the Sun, Punchao was brought outside each day and taken back inside at night. It is believed that the Inca saved Punchao, possibly their most holy religious icon, from being stolen by the Spanish by moving it in the middle of the night to their final stronghold, Vilcabamba. Archaeologists are still hoping to uncover Punchao.

The settlements of Pisaq, Huchuy Cuzco, Ollantaytambo, and Machu Picchu were placed carefully in their specific locations. Inside these constructions, carvings and sculptures were used to mark astrological events like the summer and winter solstices, by casting shadows on walls or aligning with celestial bodies.

Three symbols that show up in Inca mythology are the llama, serpent, and puma.

Without written records, we don't know for sure what these animals meant to the Inca. A tour guide will tell you that the serpent represented the spirit world, the puma represented the world of the living, and the condor connected all beings with the heavens. The shapes of some of the structures in the Sacred Valley may correspond to the forms of these and other animals important to the Inca. Some see the form of a massive condor in the mountain on which Pisaq is built and a crouching puma next to a young condor in the mountains behind Machu Picchu. Whatever these symbols meant, it is clear that they were important to the way the Inca understood the universe.

Coca: The Holy Leaf

The coca plant is a low-growing bush native to Peru. The Andean people have grown coca for thousands of years. For the Inca, the leaves of the coca plant were important for health, religion, and the **economy**.

The coca leaf is chewed or brewed as a tea. A chemical in the leaf acts as a mild **stimulant**, like coffee or tea, and also a hunger **suppressant**. People chewing coca were thought to be more productive, have more energy, and need less food. Some claim that drinking a tea brewed from coca leaves can alleviate the symptoms of altitude sickness.

Priests and priestesses used the coca leaf for ceremonial purposes. Leaves scattered on the ground were "read" to make predictions about the future. The leaves were also used as offerings to **appease** the Inca Gods.

WORDS TO KNOW

economy: the resources and wealth of a country or empire.

stimulant: a substance that increases energy levels.

suppressant: something that prevents an event from happening.

appease: to please someone by giving in to their demands.

Since money did not exist in the Inca world, valuable items like coca played an important role in trade.

Most of the cultures conquered by the Inca chewed coca and so the Inca carefully cultivated, stored, and controlled the distribution of the leaves.

BE A SAPA INCA FOR AN HOUR

The ruler of the Inca Empire was considered to be, at least in part, not of this Earth. Part of this belief meant that everything he touched in his daily life was collected, saved, and later destroyed. Since you don't have a court full of servants attending to you, it would be impossible for you to collect everything you touch in a day. But you could choose a part of the day during which you catalog every single thing you touch. See how long your list gets and think about how difficult it would be to collect these things. Where would you store them before destroying them? You would need new things every day because you could not use anything twice!

After School:
doorknob
backpack
shoes
mom
max - my dog
chair
glass of milk
snack
plate

→ SUPPLIES ←

- paper
- pencil

1 Choose a busy part of your day to conduct this experiment.

2 Over the course of an hour or two, write down every single thing you touch, such as plates, doorknobs, chairs, clothing, books, etc.

3 How long does your list get? How much space would you need to store all the things you touched?

The Spiritual Worlds of the Inca

The Inca believed in three separate spiritual worlds. Uku Pacha (the past and the interior world), Kay Pacha (the world of the present and of here), and Hanan Pacha (the future and heavenly world). Instead of thinking of these worlds as a timeline, the Inca thought of them as circles that shared a common center. People—the living, the dead, and the not yet born—were thought to be able to inhabit any of these worlds.

BREW HERBAL TEA

The Inca had a deep understanding of the medicinal properties of plants and herbs. Teas, powders, drinks, and ointments were made from naturally occurring plants to cure illnesses, improve health, and to relieve pain. The mint leaf has been used in the Andes for thousands of years to make a calming tea that some people believe helps cure an upset stomach.

Hint: This activity uses a stove, so ask an adult for help.

SUPPLIES

- fresh mint leaves
- boiling water
- coffee mug and saucer

1 Place five fresh mint leaves in a large mug. Fresh mint can be purchased at most grocery stores.

2 Fill the cup with boiling water and cover the top with a saucer.

3 Let the leaves sit in the hot water for 10 minutes before you try the tea. Enjoy this refreshing, calming tea but be careful—it may still be very hot!

CHAPTER 4

☀ Festivals and Food

The Inca depended on the natural world for all of their food, clothing, shelter, and warmth. The cycles of the moon, the sun, and the stars guided them through their planting seasons. The Inca paid respect to the natural world by organizing feasts and festivals in its honor every month of the year. The most important festivals were called *raymi*, the Quechua word for celebration. The Inti Raymi, or Festival of the Sun, was the most important religious celebration of the year.

Inti Raymi

Have you ever celebrated the **winter solstice** or the **summer solstice**? The Inti Raymi honored the sun god during the South American winter solstice in June. A Spanish **cleric** named Bartolomé de Segovia observed the Inti Raymi. He saw 600 Inca lords standing side by side in two long lines at dawn. As the sun rose, the Sapa Inca led a chant that grew louder and louder until noon, when the sun was directly overhead. As the sun moved west across the sky, the chant grew more and more quiet. Finally at sunset the singing ended, and the Inca begged the sun to come back again.

The Inti Raymi ritual lasted eight or nine days. Then the Sapa Inca welcomed the planting season by leading the people in plowing the land.

Qhapaq Raymi

The second most important celebration of the Inca year marked the South American summer solstice, which took place in December, the first month of the Inca calendar. During Qhapaq Raymi, the Magnificent Festival, teenage sons of the Inca **nobility** in Cuzco went through a month-long **rite of passage**.

WORDS TO KNOW

winter solstice: the day of the year with the least amount of sunlight.

summer solstice: the day of the year with the greatest amount of sunlight.

cleric: a leader in a church, like a minister or a priest.

nobility: considered the most important people in a society.

rite of passage: a ceremony marking an important stage in a person's life.

Did You Know?

The Spanish banned the Inti Raymi festival in 1572, but today it is held in Cuzco every year on June 24. It is the second-largest celebration in South America, smaller only than Carnaval in Rio.

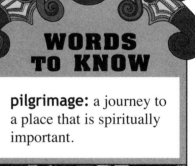

Anyone who was not a member of the Inca nobility had to leave the city. For those staying in the city, Qhapaq Raymi included **pilgrimages** to Inca holy places, sacrifices of llamas and alpacas, and a series of daring tests of skill and bravery. One highlight was a running race down the face of a mountain with young girls encouraging the teenage competitors with cups of *chicha* at the finish line. At the end of the month, the boys received gifts from their male relatives and were marked as Inca ambassadors by having large discs inserted into their earlobes.

Public ceremonies included drinking *chicha* and dancing to the music of drums and pan flutes called *zampoñas*. Everyone ate cakes made of ground corn and llama blood.

WORDS TO KNOW

pilgrimage: a journey to a place that is spiritually important.

Did You Know?

The Spanish called the Inca ambassadors *orejones* (or-ay-ho-nays) because of the large discs in their earlobes. *Orejon* means "big-ear" in Spanish. *Orejones* kept tabs on important aspects of communities throughout the empire, including the population and work capacity of each settlement, its production of crops and goods, and its devotion to the religious beliefs of the Inca.

Marking the Sun

Around the rim of Cuzco are stone markers that may have been used to identify the spring **equinox**, or a specific sunrise in the month of September at the start of the planting season.

One of the Inca's most famous solar observation devices is found at Machu Picchu in a building called the Torreón (tor-ay-own). Archaeologists discovered that a **plumb bob** hanging from the center of one of its windows cast a shadow that lined up perfectly with the edge of a cut stone on the ground on a certain day in June, marking the day of the spring equinox.

Citua

Citua was a festival focused on purification and cleansing at the start of Cuzco's rainy season in September. This was a time when many people got sick from lingering cold winter temperatures that combined with the dampness of the incoming rains.

Part of this festival involved carrying ashes from the Temple of the Sun in the four directions of the empire, Chinchaysuyu (North), Antisuyu (East), Kollasuyu (South), and Cuntisuyu (West).

WORDS TO KNOW

equinox: two days of the year, around March 21 and September 21, when there are equal hours of day and night everywhere in the world.

plumb bob: a weight suspended from a string that creates a line perfectly perpendicular to the horizon.

The ashes left the Temple of the Sun in the hands of high-level priests and were passed off to people of lower and lower class levels as they moved away from the center of the city. The last people to receive the ashes then bathed in one of the four major rivers to rid Cuzco and its population of sickness and disease.

Comets and Eclipses

Even though the Inca understood the cycles of the sun and moon, events like comets and eclipses took them by surprise. A comet is a ball of ice and dust that orbits the sun. It looks like a ball of light with a long tail when seen from Earth. An eclipse is when light is blocked from one celestial object by another one moving between it and the sun. In a lunar eclipse, Earth passes between the sun and the moon, casting a shadow on the moon. In a solar eclipse, the moon moves between the sun and Earth, blocking the sun's light. The Inca believed the sun went into mourning during a solar eclipse. To cheer up the sun, the Inca sacrificed children and livestock. They thought a giant snake or puma eating the moon caused a lunar eclipse. The Inca reacted to comets and eclipses by making a tremendous amount of noise—shouting, beating drums, blowing trumpets, making dogs howl, and throwing weapons up at the sky.

The Inca Diet: Vegetables, Grains, and a Dash of Meat

The Inca were highly advanced in large-scale farming. Having a rainy season and a dry season met their growing needs perfectly. During the rainy season the Inca ate fresh crops and plants as they grew, and during the dry season they ate crops they had dried and preserved.

INCA DIET

The Inca's excellent systems for growing and storing food had a lot to do with their success. They were never at risk of starvation, even in years when crops failed because of too much rain, too little rain, or diseases.

Have you ever climbed a very tall mountain? Living at high altitude is hard work for the human body. At an altitude of 13,000 feet (4,000 meters), there is 40 percent less oxygen in the air than at sea level! The body's primary **adaptation** to high-altitude living is to speed up its **metabolism**. A faster metabolism needs good "fuel" to keep it running.

The easiest foods for the body to harness for energy are **carbohydrates** *and the crops that the Inca cultivated were full of them.*

WORDS TO KNOW

adaptation: a change that a living thing makes to become better suited to its environment.

metabolism: the processes, like heart rate and digestion, that occur within living things in order for them to stay alive.

carbohydrate: a chemical compound in foods that contains sugar and starch.

The Inca Calendar

The calendar we use today is based on the cycles of the sun. It has 365 days. Our calendar is called the Gregorian calendar and was adopted in Europe in 1582. The Inca based their calendar on the cycles of both the sun and the moon. The annual Inca calendar was based on the daily movements of the sun, while the schedule of Inca festivals and holidays was based on the cycles of the moon. This was a bit of a problem since the lunar year is about 11 days shorter than the solar year. Historians think the Inca probably used 30-day months throughout the year, and when the holidays and seasons got out of alignment, they made adjustments to the solar calendar to get back on track.

Did You Know?

The time it takes the earth to travel once around the sun is actually slightly longer than 365 days. It is in fact 365 days, 5 hours, 48 minutes, and 46 seconds. That's why we add an extra day to February every fourth year, and we call this a leap year. If we didn't make this adjustment, our calendar would be off by 24 days every 100 years!

Plenty of Potatoes

Do you love french fries? South America is the first place in the world where potatoes were grown for food. Hundreds of years before freeze-drying was developed for things like space travel and backpacking, the Inca devised a way to freeze-dry potatoes. They used the low **humidity**, hot sun, and cold nights of the dry season to make two styles of freeze-dried potatoes called *ch'uñu* (choon-yoo) and *moraya*.

WORDS TO KNOW

humidity: the amount of moisture in the air.

First, raw potatoes soaked in a container of cold water. The women stomped on the potatoes in their bare feet (brrr!), then the potatoes were left out overnight to partially freeze. The next day, the potatoes were dried on a woven blanket in the blazing, high-altitude sun. After repeating this for three or four days, the potatoes lost all their moisture and resembled stones. The freeze-dried potatoes could be reconstituted just like powdered soup or powdered mashed potatoes by dropping them into boiling water.

Watia

Watia (wah-tee-yah) is a traditional Andean method of cooking potatoes that is still practiced ceremonially today. Clumps of soil are stacked to make a dome like a small dirt igloo. A very hot fire is lit inside the dome. As the fire dies down, potatoes are tossed into the watia and the oven is smashed down onto the potatoes. After about half an hour, the diners dig through the hot embers to find the cooked potatoes. Food cooked in an oven like this has a slightly smokey flavor and is very moist and tender.

Choclo and *Chicha*

The Inca also grew a large-kernel corn called choclo, similar to the North American corn called hominy. *Choclo* is still grown in the Andes. It was preserved in **granaries** and **silos** made of stone and **adobe**.

The Inca chose the sites for these storage buildings carefully, placing them in locations with little moisture, direct sunshine, and strong winds. The sun and wind helped to draw moisture out of the *choclo*. Along the Urubamba River, across the valley from the ruins of Ollantaytambo, one of the best examples of these granaries still stands today.

WORDS TO KNOW

granary: a building or room used to store grain.

silo: a tower used to store grain.

adobe: a building material made of sun-dried clay and straw, commonly used in areas of little rainfall.

Chicha is a beer made from corn that is still popular today in Peru, Ecuador, and Bolivia. To make *chicha*, dried corn was ground, moistened in the *chicha* maker's mouth, and spit into a pot.

This process transforms the starch in the corn into a form of sugar called maltose. The corn is combined with water and boiled. The mixture is left to sit in large ceramic pots partially buried in the ground until it ferments. *Chicha* has some alcohol content, and was consumed in massive quantities by the Inca during religious festivals.

Today you can find *chicha* in neighborhoods throughout the Andes at *chicherias*, which are bars that specialize in making the drink. Once their *chicha* is ready, the owners of the *chicheria* hang a red flag from their door so people know to come in.

Quinoa

Quinoa (keen-wah), a seed native to South America, was a mainstay of the Inca diet. It remains a popular ingredient in Andean cooking today. The dried seeds are boiled and can be eaten on their own, like rice, or in soups and stews.

Did You Know?

What we call "jerky" comes from the Quechua word *charki* (char-kee). The Inca made *charki* from the meat of alpacas, llamas, and ducks. They cut the meat into strips, which they salted and dried. This preserved the meat and made it lighter and easier to carry.

The Inca name for quinoa was chisaya mama, *which means "mother of all grains."*

Quinoa is a remarkable food. Just one cup of cooked quinoa has vitamins, amino acids, and 15 percent of the protein and 20 percent of the fiber an adult needs in a day.

MAKE YOUR OWN
ZAMPOÑA

The *zampoña* (also known as the pan flute or pan pipes) is a traditional Andean instrument that was used extensively by the Inca. It consists of a grouping of tubes, made from the dried stalks of plants that are open on one end and are cut to different lengths. When the musician blows across the open end of each tube it sounds a note that corresponds to its length. Longer tubes make lower notes, and shorter tubes make higher notes.

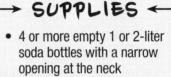

SUPPLIES

- 4 or more empty 1 or 2-liter soda bottles with a narrow opening at the neck
- water
- duct tape

1 Practice making a sound by blowing across the top of an empty bottle. Close your mouth and turn the corners of your lips up in a smile. Now just open your lips a little bit, without opening your jaws too much, and blow across the top of the bottle. You should hear a sound like a breathy whistle.

2 Fill three of the bottles with varying amounts of water to create different notes. What happens when you put more water in a bottle? What sound does it make? What sound does a bottle with less water make?

3 Once you have the notes you like, tape the four bottles together so they can be carried easily. Now you can walk around the house serenading your friends and family!

Did You Know?

Why does the amount of water in the bottle affect the sound you make? Blowing across the bottle produces sound waves that vibrate in the air in the bottle. Adding water to the bottle takes away some of the space for the sound waves to vibrate.

MAKE YOUR OWN
CH'UÑU

The Inca lived in a high **alpine** environment. This landscape offered many challenges to growing food, but the Inca used it to their advantage. For example, in the high mountains around the city of Cuzco, there are typically 300 nights of freezing temperatures every year. The Inca used these frosts to preserve their food.

SUPPLIES

- 6 small potatoes, 2 inches or smaller in diameter (5 centimeters)
- freezer
- cookie sheet
- oven (depending on the climate where you live)

1 Scrub the potatoes in cold water to remove any dirt. Place them in the freezer on a shelf and let them freeze completely overnight.

2 Remove the potatoes from the freezer and place them on the cookie sheet. If there is a warm, sunny place in your house, place them there. If you don't have a good spot, have an adult set your oven on "warm" and put the potatoes in there to dry for one hour per day.

3 Allow the potatoes to thaw completely. They will be mushy and wet. Once they are thawed, squeeze them in your hands to wring out the moisture. You should squeeze hard enough that water drips from them.

4 Use your fingernails to scrape the skin off the potatoes. If you have larger potatoes, you will need to break them into smaller pieces.

5 Return the potatoes to the freezer and allow them to freeze overnight again. Remove them the next morning and allow them to thaw again. Squeeze any moisture out. There will be less and less as you continue the process. Repeat the process for an entire week.

6 When your ch'uñu are around one quarter of the original size of the potato and look like little grey rocks, they're ready.

7 Ch'uñu are prepared for eating by boiling them in water or soup until they are soft to the touch. They will not look or taste like fresh potatoes, but they are considered a delicacy in the Andes.

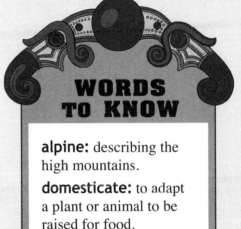

WORDS TO KNOW

alpine: describing the high mountains.

domesticate: to adapt a plant or animal to be raised for food.

Did You Know?

The people of the South American continent **domesticated** the plant that would become the potato around 8,000 years ago. There are now more than 4,500 varieties of potatoes in Peru alone. All potatoes, anywhere in the world, can be traced back to the original domesticated plant that came from South America.

MAKE YOUR OWN
CHARKI

The Inca dried their meat using naturally occurring salt, the hot sun, and the dry winds of the altiplano. Here is a recipe for *charki* that you can make using a warm oven to simulate the heat of the **equatorial** sun.

Be Careful: This activity uses both an oven and a sharp knife, so ask an adult to help.

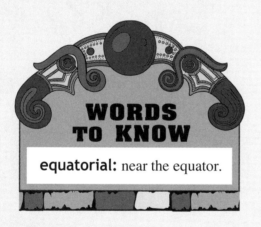

1 Wrap the beef in plastic wrap and freeze 30 to 60 minutes until firm, but not rock hard. This makes it easier to slice evenly. Ask an adult to use a sharp knife to slice the beef into strips about ¼-inch thick (just over ½ centimeter).

→ SUPPLIES ←

- 1 pound boneless top round steak or London broil, trimmed of fat (about 450 grams)
- plastic wrap
- freezer
- sharp knife
- ¼ cup soy sauce (60 milliliters)
- ¼ cup Worcestershire sauce (60 milliliters)
- ½ teaspoon salt (about 1 ½ grams)
- 1 teaspoon freshly ground black pepper (2 grams)
- ½ teaspoon garlic powder (1½ grams)
- ½ teaspoon onion powder (1½ grams)
- ziplock bag
- refrigerator
- oven
- paper towels
- broiler pan
- baking pan

2 Place soy sauce, Worcestershire sauce, salt, pepper, garlic powder, and onion powder in a large ziplock freezer bag. Seal and squish to mix.

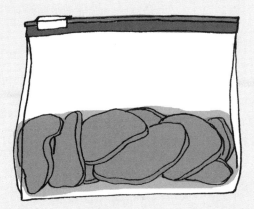

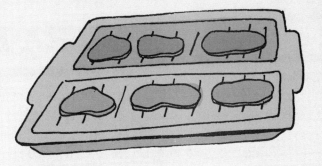

6 Arrange the beef strips on the broiler pan in a single layer with room in between for air circulation. Bake them for about 6 hours, at which point they should be dry to the touch.

7 Remove the *charki* from the oven and let it air-dry in a cool place for another 24 hours. You can store your *charki* in any airtight container. Enjoy!

3 Place the beef strips in the marinade, reseal the bag, and turn over and over to coat. Open the bag, squeeze out all of the air, reseal, and squish the mixture around. Refrigerate for 12 hours or overnight.

4 Ask an adult to preheat the oven to 175 degrees Fahrenheit (80 degrees Celsius).

5 Pull the meat strips from the marinade and pat them dry with paper towels. Place a broiler pan (with slits on it) on top of a sheet pan. The sheet pan should be bigger than the broiler pan so juices drip into it and not into your oven!

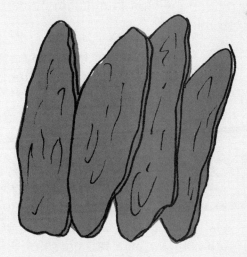

MAKE YOUR OWN
CHICHA MORADA

A variation of *chicha* that has become popular in Peru as a soft drink is called Chicha Morada. Instead of using the yellow corn kernels that the ceremonial Chicha de Jora is made from, Chicha Morada uses purple corn and is a sweet-tasting, non-alcoholic drink. It is consumed in much the same way as North Americans consume lemonade. In Peru, you can even buy Chicha Morada–flavored ice cream! You will need to buy a package of dried purple corn, which should be available at Latin American grocery stores or from a vendor on the Internet.

Be Careful: This activity involves using a stove, so make sure you ask an adult for help.

1 Combine the water, corn, cinnamon sticks, and cloves in a large pot. Bring the mixture to a boil and then reduce the heat to medium. Simmer for 40 minutes.

2 Remove the pot from the heat and carefully pour it through a strainer to remove the corn and the spices. Discard the contents of the strainer.

3 Stir the lemon juice and the sugar into the *chicha* until the sugar has dissolved. Pour the *chicha* into a tall container with a cover. Refrigerate until cold. **Enjoy a tall glass of Chicha Morada with ice!**

SUPPLIES

- large pot
- 1 gallon water (3.8 liters)
- 15 ounces purple corn (maiz morado) (425 grams)
- 2 cinnamon sticks
- 1 tablespoon whole cloves
- mesh strainer
- bowl
- wooden spoon
- 5 lemons, juiced
- 1½ cups brown sugar (330 grams)
- tall container with cover
- refrigerator

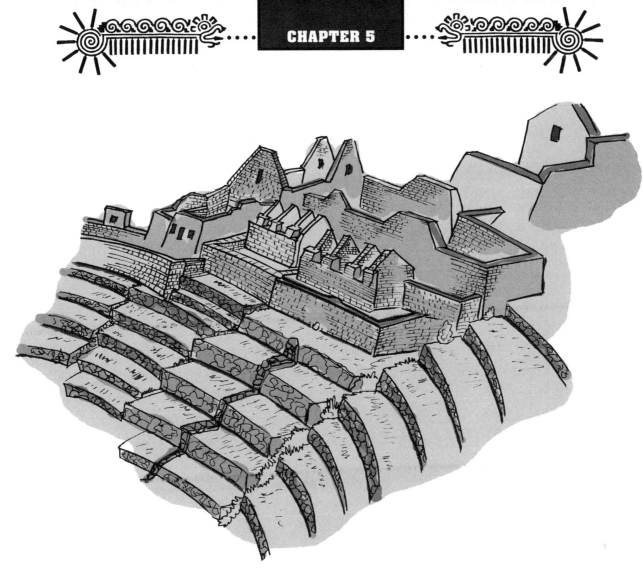

CHAPTER 5

☀ Cities and Architecture

The mountainous terrain of the Peruvian Andes, where the Inca chose to base their empire, is an unforgiving place to build things. The altitude is high, the weather and temperatures are extreme, and the land is steep. Yet this is where the Inca were able to plan, design, and construct their elaborate cities, towns, and buildings. They took some of the **innovations** of their predecessors, and made them almost perfect.

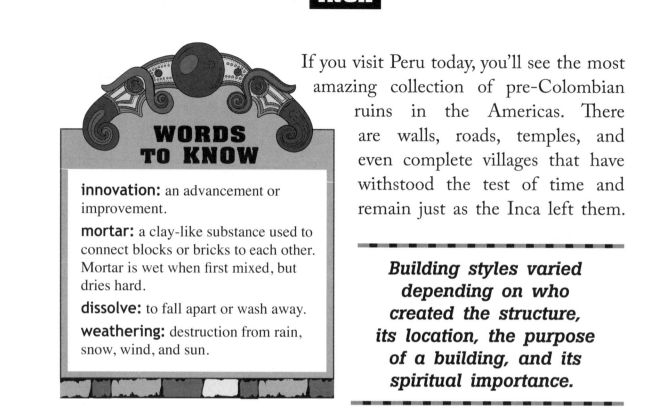

WORDS TO KNOW

innovation: an advancement or improvement.

mortar: a clay-like substance used to connect blocks or bricks to each other. Mortar is wet when first mixed, but dries hard.

dissolve: to fall apart or wash away.

weathering: destruction from rain, snow, wind, and sun.

If you visit Peru today, you'll see the most amazing collection of pre-Colombian ruins in the Americas. There are walls, roads, temples, and even complete villages that have withstood the test of time and remain just as the Inca left them.

Building styles varied depending on who created the structure, its location, the purpose of a building, and its spiritual importance.

Adobe

Adobe was the cheapest building material of the Inca. This combination of mud and straw, which turns hard once it dries, made adobe the easiest building material to use. It's a low-cost building material still used by many people in South America. Adobe is used as **mortar** to hold stones together, and used to make building blocks that can be stacked to create walls.

Because adobe **dissolves** when it gets wet, few Inca structures made of this material survived the centuries of **weathering** for us to see today. But there are a few notable exceptions.

Across the valley from the royal estate at Ollantaytambo, there is a cluster of three narrow buildings containing 10 chambers each. They are grouped together on a small step in the middle of a sheer cliff face. These narrow buildings, built of small stones held together in places with adobe, were silos used to dry and store corn. They remain standing today because they were built in a windy, dry location, protected from the rain. The Inca grew their corn in the valley near the banks of the Urubamba River. After harvesting and drying the corn, they carried it up the cliff face to pile it into the silos for storage.

Stone

The detailed stonework produced by the Inca is one of the most astounding accomplishments of the pre-Columbian world. Without metal tools or the wheel, they were able to construct walls and buildings of stunning **scale**, **precision**, beauty, and **durability**.

WORDS TO KNOW

scale: the size of something.
precision: accuracy.
durability: how well something lasts over time.

63

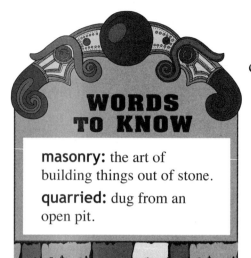

WORDS TO KNOW

masonry: the art of building things out of stone.

quarried: dug from an open pit.

Creating Inca **masonry** took a great deal of effort and skill. There are many different styles found in the ruins of Inca construction. Do you remember that, as part of their strategy for managing the empire, the Inca required their subjects to pay taxes or tribute to the government? This tax was often paid in the form of labor. Different groups of masons often came from far and wide to work on buildings together.

Saqsaywaman

One of the most impressive examples of Inca masonry is at the ruin of Saqsaywaman, perched above Cuzco at the head of the valley. Colossal blocks of stone were **quarried** about 3 miles away and moved to the site (5 kilometers). It is estimated that some of these blocks weighed more than 300,000 pounds (140 metric tons)! The blocks of stone were shaped more carefully at the site, and fit together so precisely that a piece of paper cannot slide between them. Some believe the jagged form of Saqsaywaman's walls, which zig-zag back and forth for over 1,000 feet (300 meters), represent bolts of lightning and the head and teeth of a puma.

Based on the accounts of early Spanish settlers, Saqsaywaman originally had three large towers and many interior rooms. A Spaniard named Pedro Cieza de León wrote that there was enough room in the complex to hold as many as 5,000 people! Archaeologists seem to agree that Saqsaywaman was built for a variety of uses including ceremonies, religious observation, and military equipment. It was also used as a cemetery and as a fortress for the city.

Some Inca walls consist of similar blocks about the size of a large loaf of bread, layered with surfaces bulging out slightly like pillows. Others have blocks with perfectly flat, smooth surfaces.

There are some walls with graceful curves, and others that consist of enormous stones of all different shapes, molded together perfectly like huge pieces of clay.

Did You Know?

On the street known as Hatun Rumiyoc near the center of Cuzco, is the **remnant** of a long Inca wall made of giant blocks of carved stone. One stone along the wall is especially famous. Its 12 different angles fit perfectly with the stones around it!

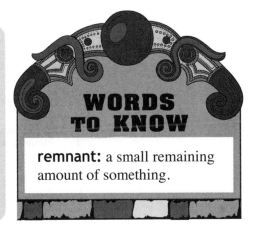

WORDS TO KNOW

remnant: a small remaining amount of something.

Cuzco: The Heart of the Inca Universe

The centerpiece of the Inca civilization was Cuzco, a compact city built inside a bowl-shaped valley facing the southwest. The city was made up of royal palaces, houses for the various levels of the Inca nobility, temples, and plazas.

The city was redesigned and rebuilt by the Sapa Inca Pachacuti. He had some of the existing buildings destroyed before beginning his massive project in the early 1400s. The city was precisely laid out and very deliberately organized.

Cuzco's shape and scale were closely tied to both the constellations in the night sky and the physical features in the landscape. Certain places on the landscape were considered sacred shrines and were called *waq'a* (wock-ahh). A *waq'a* could be a mountain peak, rock formation, spring, irrigation channel, temple, storehouse, or palace (among other things).

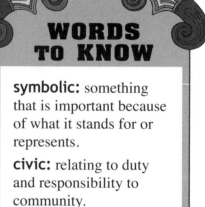

WORDS TO KNOW

symbolic: something that is important because of what it stands for or represents.

civic: relating to duty and responsibility to community.

The K'oricancha in Cuzco, or Temple of the Sun, was the centerpoint for a system of **symbolic** lines known as the *zeq'e* lines. More than 40 of these lines fanned out from the K'oricancha like the spokes of a wheel. They touched many *waq'as* along their paths.

Experts believe these lines were part of a complex system that served many connected purposes. The lines may have described the class level and relatedness of families or the dates of important events in Inca history. They could have related to the timing of astrological events (like the solstices), the control of water from irrigation channels, and the distribution of labor and **civic** responsibilities.

Earthquake-Proofing

The land where the Inca built their empire was and still is **seismically** active. This means it is a place where earthquakes are likely to happen. The Inca knew their buildings might be shaken at any moment by violent movements in the land.

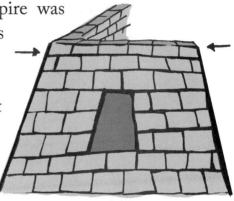

Unlike the walls of modern constructions, most Inca walls tilted inward, toward the center of the building. This meant that each face of a rectangular building was actually a **trapezoid**. Doorways, windows, and **niches** were also made in the shape of trapezoids. The Inca architects knew that the **obtuse** and **acute angles** in a trapezoid were more stable than the **right angles** of a rectangle.

WORDS TO KNOW

seismic: relating to earthquakes.

trapezoid: a four-sided shape with two parallel sides.

niche: a shallow recess in a wall.

obtuse angle: an angle greater than 90 degrees.

acute angle: an angle smaller than 90 degrees.

right angle: an angle that measures exactly 90 degrees, like at the corner of a square or rectangle.

fault: a crack in the outer layer of the earth where two different plates meet.

Did You Know?

On a ridge just above the city of Cuzco, there is a visible trench in the land that runs all the way to the ruins of Machu Picchu. This trench is called the Tambo Machay **fault** and was the location of major earthquakes in the region in 1950 and 1986.

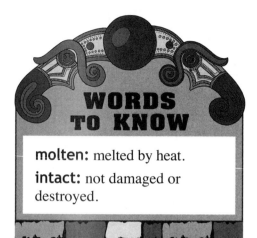

There is also evidence that the Inca devised a system to link blocks of rock together using **molten** metal. Some unfinished walls have T-shaped grooves on their top surfaces, and bordering blocks are arranged so that the openings of these grooves line up with each other. The theory is that once the stones were in place, molten copper or bronze was poured into the grooves, which cooled and hardened to hold the two blocks together.

Machu Picchu

Without a doubt, one of the most important archaeological finds of all time is the stunning mountaintop estate of the Inca royalty, called Machu Picchu. Discovered in 1911 by Hiram Bingham, a professor at Yale University, the settlement had never been seen by any non-Andean person before local guides led Bingham up its steep slopes. When Bingham arrived, Machu Picchu was covered in hundreds of years of vegetation, but was otherwise **intact**. Since its location is so remote, the Spanish never found Machu Picchu. If they had discovered it, it's likely they would have destroyed it in their desperate search for items made of gold and silver.

HUAYNA PICCHU

SACRED ROCK

PRINCIPAL TEMPLE

TEMPLE OF 3 WINDOWS

MORTARS

TEMPLE OF THE CONDOR

ROYAL PALACE

ROYAL PALACE

TEMPLE OF THE SUN

Machu Picchu sits on the top of a steep ridge whose top has been flattened. It sits high above the Urubamba River, which turns in a series of **oxbows** almost completely around it. The original entrance to the complex is a narrow land bridge, descending from the ridge system above.

> *It would have been nearly impossible for attackers to get through its gates unnoticed.*

WORDS TO KNOW

oxbow: a U-shaped bend in a river.

urban: relating to cities or towns.

granite: a type of rock that contains many crystals. It is formed underground over a long period of time with an enormous amount of pressure.

Like other royal estates, Machu Picchu had a natural spring, with fresh water bubbling out of the ground. Some water was taken from its source and sent along carved stone channels to the **urban** sector for residents to drink and bathe in. Water used to irrigate crops was delivered to the many terraces in the agricultural sector that were built into the sheer cliffs hanging thousands of feet above the river.

The ridge that Machu Picchu sits on is a huge mass of **granite**. Even though it looks solid, there are many splits and fractures in the rock. This means parts of the ridge could move violently and independently during earthquakes. Amazingly, the Inca seemed to know about these fractures and never built on top of them.

Did You Know?

After Hiram Bingham discovered Machu Picchu in 1911, he brought thousands of ceramic, stone, and gold objects he found there back to Yale University, where he was a professor. A hundred years later, Yale is returning the treasures to Cuzco.

Machu Picchu is full of unique stone creations, such as the Temple of the Condor. Below a small **knoll** there is an area of solid granite that has been cut away on one side to create a hollow space inside it. Two **buttresses** were left intact, which rise like the wings of a bird from the ground toward the top of the knoll.

Flat on the ground in front of these "wings," the head and neck of a condor are carved into stone. The space inside has many niches carved into the walls.

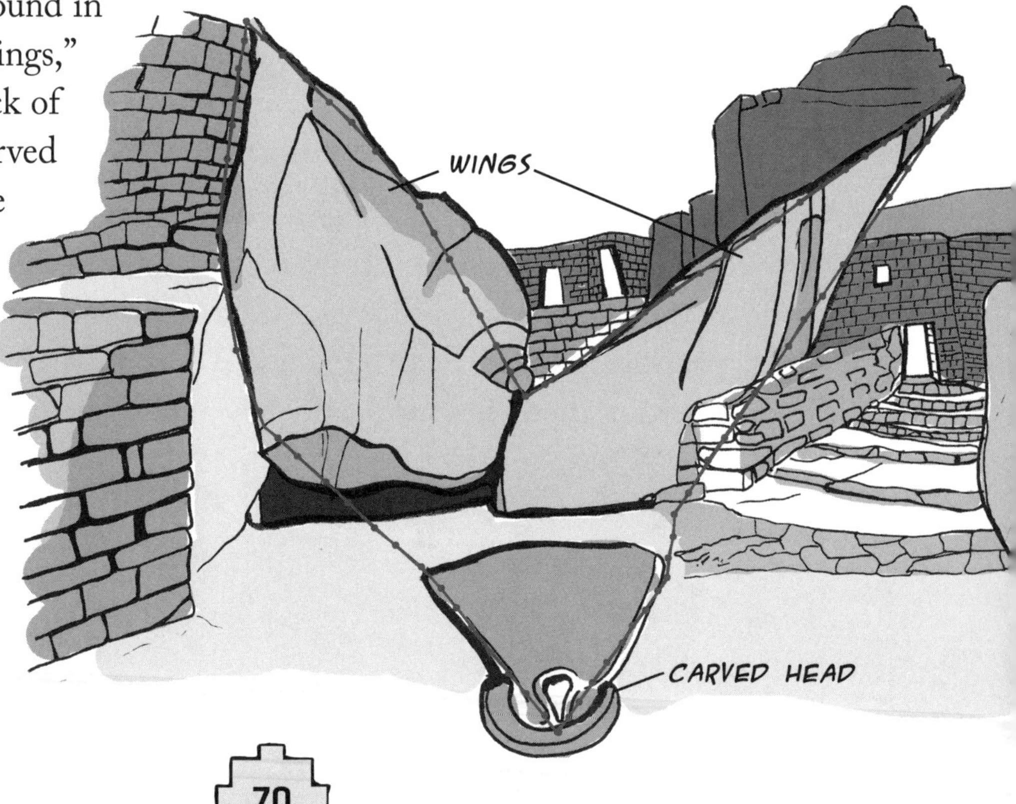

WORDS TO KNOW

knoll: a small round hill.

buttress: a support in a building that projects out from a wall.

WINGS

CARVED HEAD

It's no surprise that a number of sites high atop Machu Picchu were designed as observatories for watching and recording the movements of the sun, moon, planets, and stars.

Above the Temple of the Condor is a cave called the Intimachay. This cave has walls made of Inca masonry blocks, with a window carved into a boulder on one side. The cave was built so the light during sunrise falls on the back wall for 10 days before and 10 days after the winter solstice.

Irrigation

Plants need water to grow and people need water to live. The Inca celebrated and worshipped water. They created elaborate systems to move water through their fields, cities, temples, and palaces.

In the village of Ollantaytambo, the irrigation systems built by the Sapa Inca Pachacuti still exist and continue to function flawlessly, almost 600 years after they were constructed! Water is diverted from the Patakancha River into a series of channels that pass across the thresholds of buildings, so the residents only have to step outside to get it. After passing through the city, the channels traverse fields of crops before spilling back into the Urubamba River. Across the valley, on Pachacuti's personal estate, is another irrigation system that is more complex and ceremonial than the one found in the village. This one includes formal baths and fountains in addition to irrigation canals.

In a number of places in the Sacred Valley, the Inca were actually able to change the course of rivers! At the village of Yucay, the river was diverted and an area of marshy riverbank was converted into agricultural land. In the area leading up to Ollantaytambo, the river was redirected to flow from one side of the valley to the other. This meant that potential invaders might have to cross the river a number of times to reach the village.

Ollantaytambo

Ollantaytambo is a complex in the Sacred Valley consisting of an estate and a village. The village is the best-preserved Inca urban area in existence. In most modern cities, the streets create blocks that are square or rectangular. But at Ollantaytambo, the streets form blocks in a shape commonly used by the Inca, the trapezoid.

The layout of Ollantaytambo's streets, irrigation canals, agricultural fields, and terraces is nearly identical to how it was during the Inca Empire.

Ollantaytambo sits at the end of the most gentle portion of the Sacred Valley. Just beyond it, the Urubamba River begins its steep descent into the jungle through tight gorges with roaring rapids. Some archaeologists believe the Inca may have chosen this location because it provided natural protection against attacks from the tribes of the Amazon jungle.

One of the most amazing structures at Ollantaytambo is the unfinished Temple of the Sun. It consists of six enormous slabs of rose-colored stone standing up on their ends side by side. The slabs are made of a type of rock containing millions of tiny quartz crystals that sparkle in the sun. The rocks were quarried more than 2 miles from Ollantaytambo (more than 3 kilometers) and some weigh more than 100,000 pounds.

How did the Inca get the stone to Ollantaytambo? No one is really sure, but it was probably a combination of brute force and **levers**, rollers, and dragging with ropes.

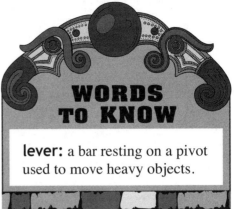

WORDS TO KNOW

lever: a bar resting on a pivot used to move heavy objects.

Pisaq

Of course the Sapa Inca Pachacuti didn't have just one estate, and the ruins of Pisaq are believed to be another of his estates. Pisaq is filled with some of the finest Inca stonework in all of South America, including temples and fountains. It also contains the Inca's largest system of agricultural terracing.

> *Without seeing it in person, it's almost impossible to picture the massive scale of the earthworks.*

The buildings of Pisaq are built on the crest of its ridge. As with all villages, the residents of Pisaq needed fresh water. The Inca built Pisaq where there was a natural spring. Along the very top of the ridge there is still an original Inca pathway with paved steps and a tunnel cut right through solid bedrock! Watch your step on this trail or you'll be falling nearly 500 feet to the bottom of the cliff (152 meters).

Agricultural Terracing

In an area characterized by steep mountainsides and periods of **torrential rain**, construction requires special preparation and innovative techniques. Many Inca establishments are built on uneven terrain with steeply angled slopes of loose dirt and gravel. To protect against **erosion** and landslides, the Inca became masters of **agricultural terracing**. But these terraces didn't just stabilize the land. They also provided a nearly perfect system for growing crops. Eventually, the Inca became such knowledgeable farmers that they were able to double their **yield** of crops on the land.

The real genius of the Inca terraces is found mostly underground. The bottom layer consists of broken rocks and gravel for good drainage. The next layer is made up of the soil that was dug up to cut the terrace into the hillside. The top layer is **nutrient**-rich soil, often dug from riverbanks and carried great distances to be placed on the terraces. Flat stones protruding from the stone walls around terraces were angled perfectly to make a series of "floating stairs" that allowed people to move easily from terrace to terrace.

WORDS TO KNOW

torrential rain: very heavy rain.

erosion: when soil, rock, and land is washed away by the effects of water, wind, and ice.

agricultural terracing: reshaping sloping land into a series of steps.

yield: the amount of a crop harvested on an area of land.

nutrient: substances in food and soil that living things need to live and grow.

IRRIGATION CANAL

NUTRIENT-RICH SOIL

SOIL

DRAINAGE (BROKEN ROCKS)

CREATE A PLUMB BOB

A plumb bob is a device used by many cultures, including the Inca, to create a line segment that is perfectly perpendicular to the level surface of the earth. The Inca used plumb bobs for construction as well as for casting shadows during important astrological events.

Hint: It's easier to do this activity with two people, so ask a friend or family member to help.

1 Tie the string to the heavy object. Go to a flat surface and have someone hold the string so the heavy object is hovering just above the surface.

2 Hold the protractor upright on the surface with its flat side down. Look at where the string intersects the protractor and read the number. It should be at 90 degrees.

3 Now go to a surface that is not level, like a hill or a ramp. Hang the plumb bob again and hold the protractor upright on the surface with the flat side down. Look again at the number on the protractor where the string intersects it. The difference between this number and 90 degrees is the angle that this surface is tipped from level. If the number you read is less than 90 degrees, subtract it from 90 degrees to get the angle. If the number you read is greater than 90 degrees, subtract 90 degrees from the number to get the angle.

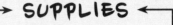

SUPPLIES

- 2 or 3 feet of kite string (½ to 1 meter)
- small, heavy object, like a nut, bolt, or fishing sinker
- semicircular protractor
- flat surface
- slanted surface

EXPLORE EROSION

One of the great challenges of building an empire in a mountainous place like the Andes Mountains is managing the steep slopes of the landscape. To fight the effects of erosion, the Inca created terraces and even diverted the flow of rivers. This activity will let you witness the effects of erosion firsthand.

1 Fill one lasagna pan with dirt. It should be 2 to 3 inches deep and cover the bottom of the pan (5 to 7½ centimeters).

2 Look at the dirt carefully with your magnifying lens. Get your hands dirty! How does the dirt feel? What do you think the dirt is made of? Write down your observations in your notebook.

3 With the scissors, poke 6 small holes in one end of the tray that is holding the dirt. Put the second tray under the end of the dirt-filled tray where the holes are.

→ SUPPLIES ←

- 2 large disposable lasagna pans
- dirt from your backyard (NOT potting soil from a bag!)
- magnifying lens
- notebook
- pencil
- scissors
- 2 or 3 thick books
- water
- watering can
- shovel (optional)

4 Slip the books under the other end of the dirt-filled try so it is propped up about 2 inches (5 centimeters). Make sure the books are not inside the catcher tray or they will get soaked! Write down in your notebook what you think will happen when you pour water on the dirt.

5 Pour water from the watering can onto the dirt. Did the appearance of the dirt in the pan change? Did some of the dirt get washed into the pan underneath? What do you think would happen if you tipped the pan more steeply? What do you think would happen if the dirt was already wet? Write down your observations and ideas.

6 Experiment with different scenarios. Try building a really steep slope to see how powerful erosion can be on the sheer mountainsides of the land of the Inca.

7 You can experiment with erosion outside by building a dirt mound where it won't be disturbed. Measure your "mountain" once a week. Build two mountains—one steeper than the other. Observe what happens over time.

INVESTIGATE

THE ADVANTAGES OF TERRACES

Many cultures, including the Inca, realized the benefits of building terraces into their mountainous terrain. This activity will demonstrate how terraces create more space in the land to grow more crops.

SUPPLIES

- 1 piece of notebook paper
- ruler
- pencil
- masking tape

1 Cut your paper the long way to make two strips, each about 4 inches wide (10 centimeters).

2 Find something in your house that has a corner with a right angle, like a framed picture or a window. Hold one strip of paper flat against the surface at a 45-degree angle so it intersects the bottom and side of the window or frame. Use tape to mark the two spots where the paper crosses the window or frame. Also mark the two spots on the paper where it crosses the window or frame. Measure this distance and label it "flat surface." Write this measurement on the strip of paper.

78

3 Now, hold the second strip of paper out horizontally to the frame or window. Starting at one tape mark, fold the paper accordion style at 90-degree angles so it makes a staircase. Keep about 2 inches between each fold (5 centimeters). Continue this until the other end of the paper reaches the second tape mark. Mark the spot on the paper where it intersects the second tape mark.

4 Unfold the paper so it is lying flat. Measure the distance from the edge of the paper to the mark you just made and label it "terraced surface." Write down this measurement on the second strip of paper.

5 Which distance was greater? The length of the flat, angled surface, or the combined length of the horizontal and vertical sections of the "terraced" piece of paper? The flat angled surface represents the available land on a sloping hillside without terracing. The terraced surface represents the available land on a terraced hillside.

MAKE YOUR OWN
SUNDIAL

The Inca used the positions of the sun, moon, stars, and planets to mark dates on their calendar and to know what the season was. In this activity, you will create a device that uses the position of the sun to tell time. Just make sure you use it on a sunny day!

SUPPLIES

- paper plate
- sharp pencil
- ruler
- crayons
- plastic straw
- duct tape
- sunny place
- clock or watch

1 Poke a hole in the center of the plate with a sharp pencil. Turn the plate upside down and write the number 12 on its edge. Use a ruler and crayon to draw a line from the 12 to the hole in the plate.

2 Put the straw in the hole and tape it in place so its end is tilted toward the 12 and the line that you drew. Put the paper plate in a sunny spot just before noon.

3 At exactly noon, turn the plate so the straw's shadow lines up perfectly with the line and the 12. Making sure not to move it, tape the plate in place.

4 At exactly 1:00 on your watch, mark the spot on the plate where the straw's shadow falls and write the number 1. Repeat this process every hour to complete the clock. You will have to fill in the morning hours the next day.

5 As long as your sundial faces the exact direction as when you made it, you can use the sundial to tell time.

CHAPTER 6

☀ Clothing and Textiles

The Inca and their predecessors were highly accomplished at spinning, weaving, and sewing. Everyone, including men, women, and children, knew how to spin raw **fibers** of cotton or wool into thread using a drop spindle. Fiber art was one of the most valued skills in the Inca Empire. The fabrics and clothes the Inca created were intricately designed and decorated with colors, patterns, and images that told stories and had religious and spiritual meaning.

Textile Production

How did the Inca choose the materials used in their textiles? Remember, the Inca Empire covered nearly 400,000 square miles at its height (1 million square kilometers). Squeezed between the Pacific Ocean on the west and the Amazon jungle on the east, the land varied in **topography** and weather. Choosing which materials to use for textiles depended on the specific climate where the textiles would be used. It also depended on what they were to be used for, and by whom.

Along the hot, dry coast, textiles were typically made of cotton grown on farms. In the cold, damp mountains, textiles were usually made of wool from llamas, alpacas, **vicuñas**, and **guanacos**. The Inca even used wool from **viscachas** and bats!

WORDS TO KNOW

fibers: long, slender threads of material such as wool or cotton that can be spun into yarn.

topography: the shape of the landscape.

vicuñas and guanacos: small Andean hoofed animals related to the camel with coats of very fine wool.

viscacha: an Andean rodent with very fine fur that looks like a rabbit. Related to the llama and alpaca.

Different types of cloth were used for different textiles. The lowest quality cloth was called *chusi* (choo-see). *Chusi* was used for blankets and other items that needed to be durable. *Awasqa* (ah-woss-ka) was the next best in quality and was the most commonly produced fabric in the empire. *Qompi* (comb-pea) was the finest fabric and was made from a mix of cotton and wool.

The finest qompi *weavings from the Andes
may contain more than 6 miles of hand-spun
and dyed thread (9½ kilometers)!*

The most elaborate *qompi* was woven with special items. These included the iridescent feathers from hummingbirds' chests, bat fur, pieces of gold and silver, or colorful shells from the coast.

To meet the tremendous demand for cloth, the Inca created a number of communities dedicated to textile production. On the altiplano near Lake Titicaca, a large settlement called Milliraya employed 1,000 weavers. In return for producing textiles, the residents were given lakefront land, irrigated fields, pastures, and fields of crops.

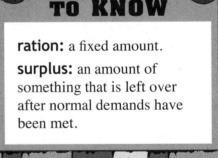

Did You Know?

In the records the Inca kept, the number of people and llamas and alpacas were listed first, followed by the quantity of textiles. Textiles were considered more important than food and gold!

WORDS TO KNOW

ration: a fixed amount.

surplus: an amount of something that is left over after normal demands have been met.

Uses of Textiles

Most of the textiles went to the Inca army. Every year, soldiers received a **ration** of clothing, blankets, and shoes made from the middle-quality cloth, *awasqa*. Storehouses along the Inca roads were filled from floor to ceiling with **surplus** items made from woven cloth.

Did You Know?

According to one historical account, storehouses near the village of Xauxa had enough **inventory** to supply the local population with everything they needed for 30 years after the collapse of the Inca Empire!

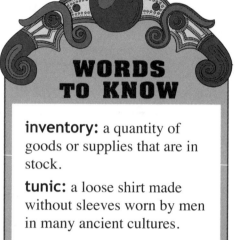

WORDS TO KNOW

inventory: a quantity of goods or supplies that are in stock.

tunic: a loose shirt made without sleeves worn by men in many ancient cultures.

Textiles were an important part of ceremonies and rituals. Large numbers of tapestries were burned in festivals and buried along with sacrifices and mummies. One upper-class marriage ritual was for the groom to travel to his bride's home, accompanied by music, to offer her a finely woven *qompi* tapestry. Her family would return the favor by giving the groom a *qompi* **tunic**, and they would both change into their new clothing right then and there.

Do you have a backpack? The Inca made their own version called a *lliqlla* (yeek-yah). It was made from two tapestries sewn together to create a large rectangle. The *lliqlla* was used to carry everything from crops, to babies, to tools, and firewood. The items were placed in the center of the *lliqlla*. Then the wearer hoisted it up and secured it by tying the two opposite corners together over one shoulder.

When the lliqlla was empty, it served as a warm extra layer, or as a ground covering for a nap or picnic.

The images and designs on Inca textiles varied greatly and had many purposes and meanings. The colors and shapes on a garment might tell where a person was from and what community that person belonged to. Some tapestries clearly depicted people, animals, and realistic scenes. Other creations had more **abstract**, geometric **representations** of animals and people that even combined at times to make invented creatures. On some weavings a crab might transform into a snake, or a human might have the head of a puma.

The Sapa Inca's tunics included many squares with geometric shapes embroidered or woven inside of them, called *tocapus* (tow-cop-ooz). Some scholars think these shapes signified the great number of diverse things in the world that the Sapa Inca ruled over, while others think it was a form of **pictorial** writing.

Types of Clothing

The Inca wore clothing that kept them comfortable and protected from the elements, with designs and colors that told the story of their **heritage** and class level.

WORDS TO KNOW

abstract: existing more in thought and ideas than in reality.

representation: a depiction of things in pictures or other forms of art.

pictorial: something expressed in pictures or art.

heritage: the cultural traditions and history of a group of people.

Men wore a rectangular tunic that went over their heads and had holes on the sides for their arms. They also wore a **loincloth**, which all men received as part of their coming-of-age ceremony around the age of 14. In colder regions the men wrapped themselves in large **cloaks**.

They also wore an **ornate**, cone-shaped hat with earflaps called a *ch'ulu* (chuh-oo-loo).

Women wrapped a rectangular cloth around their bodies and under their arms, then pinned it together over their shoulders. Around their waist they tied a woven belt called a *chumpi* (choom-pea). In the cooler regions they also wore a *lliqlla* over their shoulders when they weren't using it to carry things.

WORDS TO KNOW

loincloth: a single piece of cloth wrapped around the hips. It was worn by men in many ancient cultures as their only piece of clothing.

cloak: a garment like a cape that is worn loosely over the shoulders to provide extra warmth.

ornate: decorated intricately, with complex patterns and shapes.

Textile Museums and Workshops

Weaving is an integral part of Andean identity, a tradition that goes back thousands of years. With the development of factories, the time-consuming practice of making wool products by hand risked being lost. In the countries of Peru, Bolivia, and Ecuador, foundations have been established to promote and preserve weaving as a living art. It is now possible to visit exhibits of ancient textiles while native weavers sit on the ground in the courtyard, creating new works in the same way they have been made for centuries. In rural communities, weaving cooperatives have been established where tourists may buy textiles from the native Andeans. The promise of money in exchange for pieces of traditional weaving provides an incentive to keep the ancient skills alive.

MAKE YOUR OWN
INCA ARMY TUNIC

Inca soldiers were able to overwhelm tens of thousands of opponents in their campaign to grow their empire. Part of their success was due to their military skill, but part of it was from the way they presented themselves. The Inca terrified their enemies with their sheer numbers and matching, eye-popping uniforms. In this project you will create a replica Inca tunic with the checkerboard pattern that likely terrified enemies when they saw them approaching.

SUPPLIES

- paper bag
- scissors
- ruler
- black sharpie
- black tempera paint
- paint brush

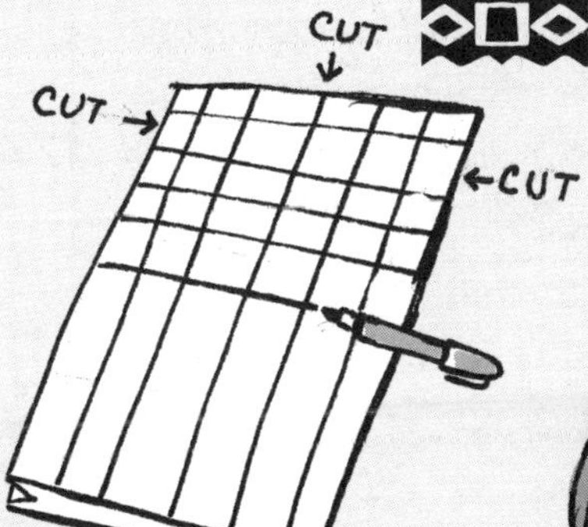

1 To make the tunic, first cut a hole in the bottom of the paper bag large enough for your head to fit through. Cut slits up the sides for your arms.

2 Now make the checkerboard design. Use the ruler and the black sharpie to make a checkerboard pattern on the front and back of the paper bag.

3 Paint every other square of the pattern on the tunic. Let the paint dry on the front, then paint the pattern on the back. The colors of the army's tunics were simple black and white—a combination that stunned enemies with its high contrast.

MAKE A
DROP SPINDLE

Drop spindles were used by many ancient cultures to spin fibers like wool and cotton into thread. They consist of a narrow shaft in the center with a round weight at one end called a whorl. After spinning the spindle like a top, you let it go while holding on to the clump of wool in one hand. The whorl gives the spindle some weight to keep it spinning and pulls the fiber down into a twisted thread. The Inca name for the drop spindle was *pushkana* (poosh-kah-nah). This project will use some modern materials, but you could make a *pushkana* completely out of items from your backyard like the Inca did!

Be Careful: Make sure an adult helps you use an oven. Also ask an adult for help if you use the knife.

SUPPLIES

- chopstick (around 12 inches or 30 centimeters long)
- ruler
- kitchen shears or small serrated knife
- 2-ounce block of oven-bake polymer clay (available at craft stores)
- cutting board
- rolling pin
- lid from a jar 2 or 3 inches in diameter (5 to 7½ centimeters)
- butter knife
- cookie sheet
- oven
- bulk wool or cotton balls

1 Cut the chopstick to length, if necessary. Measure 12 inches from the thick end and make a mark on the chopstick (30 centimeters). Cut the thin end off with a pair of kitchen shears or small serrated knife. An adult needs to help you!

2 To make the whorl, take your block of clay and lay it down on a cutting board. Measure how thick it is with a ruler. Flatten the clay with the rolling pin until it is ¼-inch thick (0.6 centimeters).

3 Press the lid into the clay to form a perfect circle. Use a butter knife to cut through the clay all the way around the lid.

4 Locate the exact center of the whorl. You can eyeball it or you can use the ruler to lightly trace two lines across the circle that intersect at the center. Carefully poke a hole in the center with the narrower end of the chopstick. Just push the chopstick through without moving it around—the clay will shrink just enough to make a tight fit after it is baked. Gently smooth the edge of the whorl where you cut it out. Be very careful to keep it round and flat so it will be balanced when it spins.

5 Place the clay disk on the cookie sheet. Bake the whorl following the instructions on the package.

6 Now you can assemble your pushkana. Wait until the whorl has cooled somewhat from baking, but is not yet room temperature. This will allow it to shrink right onto the chopstick while it cools. Just push the whorl up the chopstick until it stops. It should rest 1 or 2 inches up from the narrow end (2½ to 5 centimeters).

7 After the pushkana is finished, get some cotton balls or bulk wool and try spinning thread from them. It's much easier to work with the wool if you can get it. Pinch a small tuft between your thumb and finger and gently pull it away to start a thread. Carefully tie this tuft around the chopstick, just above the whorl. Spin the pushkana and see what happens. If it doesn't work, keep practicing. It may take you some time to get the hang of it! With practice, you can spin yarn out of a ball of fibers.

MAKE YOUR OWN
INCA T-SHIRT

The Inca made designs in their weavings and artwork that used repeating shapes and abstract representations of animals and mythical figures. Choose from the shapes shown or make up your own to create a T-shirt version of an Inca tapestry. Choose vibrant colors!

Hint: This uses a hot iron, so have an adult do the ironing. You can buy transfer paper at an office supply store.

→ SUPPLIES ←

- scrap paper
- colored pencils or permanent markers
- iron-on transfer paper
- iron
- white T-shirt

1 Typically, Andean weavings have matching borders with different shapes or images in the middle. On the scrap paper, draw the shape for your borders. Repeat the shape in a line across the page.

2 Then draw the shape you would like repeating in the center of your "tapestry." Copy one of the images shown here, or make up your own.

3 Now draw your design on the transfer paper using vibrant colored pencils or permanent markers.

4 Ask an adult to iron the transfer paper on the T-shirt for you. Iron with no steam and press down hard while moving the iron until the edges of the transfer paper start to peel away easily from the shirt. Peel the transfer paper away from the T-shirt. If color starts to come off on the transfer paper, press it down again and keep ironing until the peel comes off cleanly.

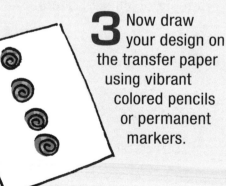

CHAPTER 7

⊚ The Spanish Conquest

It's hard to believe that a tiny group of adventurers from halfway around the globe could conquer the world's mightiest empire. But the Spanish had great timing. They arrived in the early 1500s when the Inca Empire was weak. There was a lot of fighting within the empire and many people were suffering from disease. These troubles combined with the religious fervor and greed of the Spanish. It was a lethal combination that eventually led to the collapse of the Inca world.

Who Were the Conquistadors?

The conquistadors came to Peru from the European country of Spain. Like other European countries at this time, Spain was busy trying to **colonize** the New World. Explorers convinced the king and queen of Spain to fund **expeditions** to unknown areas in hopes of discovering territories filled with riches like silver and gold.

If the explorers found the treasure they hoped for, Spain would get some of it. And the men who found it would become extremely rich.

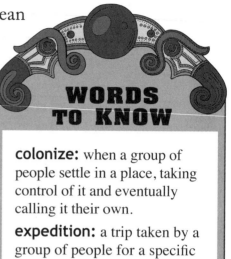

WORDS TO KNOW

colonize: when a group of people settle in a place, taking control of it and eventually calling it their own.

expedition: a trip taken by a group of people for a specific purpose like exploration, scientific research, or war.

Francisco Pizarro led the campaign that toppled the Inca. Pizarro did not have much hope for a successful life in his home country. He came from Trujillo, a poor town in the west of Spain that had a large number of thieves, bullies, and neglected children like him. Pizarro could not read. Becoming an explorer seemed like an exciting way to get out of town.

With nothing much to lose, Pizarro and other men from Trujillo travelled to the port town of Seville where they signed up for expeditions to the far corners of the planet. They hoped to find fortune, but they also knew they might die trying to get it.

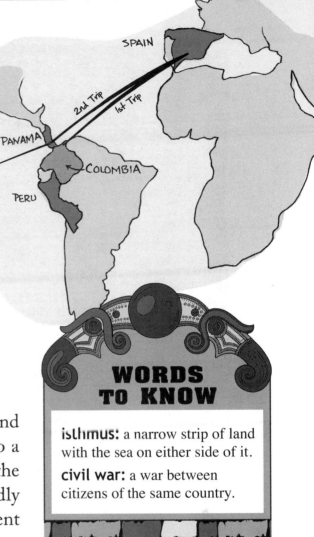

Pizarro joined an expedition to Cartagena, Colombia, in 1509, and then another to Panama in 1513. This second trip successfully crossed the narrow **Isthmus** of Panama to reach the Pacific Ocean. In return for his services, Pizarro was granted an estate in Panama and the title of Mayor of Panama City. He now had money and a perfect home base for launching explorations in South America.

Problems in the Inca Empire

As luck would have it, the powerful and unified empire of the Inca had fallen into a bitter **civil war** right around the time the Spanish arrived in Peru. Smallpox, a deadly disease, was tearing through the continent like wildfire. Earlier European explorers who landed in Mexico most likely brought it to the region. In some areas, the virus killed 90 percent of the Inca population. Smallpox killed anyone it touched. In fact, in 1527 it killed the ruling Sapa Inca Huayna Capac and his son, Ninan Cuchoyic, who would have inherited the role of Sapa Inca from his father.

WORDS TO KNOW

isthmus: a narrow strip of land with the sea on either side of it.

civil war: a war between citizens of the same country.

A fight then broke out between two other sons of Wayna Qhapaq over who should be the next Sapa Inca.

The Conquistadors Are Coming

After hearing reports of a vast empire filled with great riches in South America, Francisco Pizarro focused on getting himself there. He knew this was probably his best and final chance to become wildly rich and powerful. Early trips to find the Inca Empire were difficult, with many men dying from disease. On one of these trips his men intercepted a balsa-wood raft carrying native people with gold and silver figurines and beautifully woven tapestries and clothing. Back in Panama, Pizarro tried to convince a group of men to go back and conquer the whole continent, but he had no luck. So in 1525, Pizarro sailed back to Spain and shared his tales of the riches of Peru with King Charles and Queen Isabella. The king and queen gave Pizarro their royal blessing to invade the land. They agreed that one-fifth of any riches Pizarro found would go to Spain and he could keep the rest for himself and his men.

While Pizarro prepared to invade, Huascar and Atahualpa fought for the Inca throne from 1527 to 1532. Huascar was the highest-ranking Inca in Cuzco at the time of his father's death, while Atahualpa was the highest-ranking Inca in Quitu (now known as the city of Quito in Ecuador).

Huascar declared himself the Sapa Inca, but Atahualpa and his army were heading to Cuzco to confront Huascar and claim the title of Sapa Inca. In 1532, Atahualpa's forces captured Huascar and killed him. But Atahualpa's **reign** would end almost as quickly as it began. While celebrating in the town of Cajamarca (ka-ha-mark-ah), he was discovered by Francisco Pizarro and his team of 160 men.

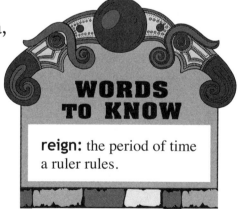

WORDS TO KNOW

reign: the period of time a ruler rules.

Did You Know?

The Inca Empire had expanded so much that it was becoming more and more difficult to manage. But with the spread of smallpox and the death of so many people, the Inca Empire began to break apart.

Two Worlds Collide

Pizarro and his men had landed on the coast of Peru for the third time on May 16, 1532. Pizarro's small army consisted of around 100 men on foot and 60 more on horseback. The men were both scared and excited as they followed an Inca road through extremely rugged terrain. On Friday, November 15, 1532, after crossing a vast grassland at 13,500 feet (over 4,000 meters), the Spaniards looked down onto the rolling valley of Cajamarca. The hills surrounding the town were sprinkled with Inca army tents as far as the eye could see.

Atahualpa knew the Spaniards were coming, but he wasn't too worried about them. After all, the Inca army under Atahualpa's command had nearly 500 times more soldiers than the Spanish, and they were fierce warriors. The Spanish knew they were vastly outnumbered and decided that they must not show any signs of fear to their enemies. Even

though they were terrified, Pizarro and his men pretended to march confidently into the center of Cajamarca. They sent a small group to the royal palace to request a meeting with the Sapa Inca, Atahualpa.

What happened next was such a bold act that it marked the beginning of the end of the Inca Empire. The plan Pizarro and his men put into action started a chain of events that would eventually topple the great Inca civilization.

The plaza in the center of Cajamarca was surrounded on three sides by buildings, with a narrow gate in a wall on the fourth side.

The Spaniards' plan hinged on Atahualpa coming to meet them in the town square, so they could ambush him in an enclosed space.

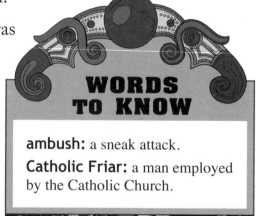

WORDS TO KNOW

ambush: a sneak attack.

Catholic Friar: a man employed by the Catholic Church.

Some Spanish soldiers hid with small cannons in the buildings around the plaza. The group stayed up all night planning their

attack. Atahualpa was carried to town on his elaborate litter, accompanied by around 5,000 soldiers. The Spanish were terrified at the sight! As the Sapa Inca entered the plaza, he was surprised not to find it filled with Spaniards. He called out, "Where are they?" and as he did, a **Catholic Friar** named Vicente de Valverde came out of one of the buildings holding a cross in one hand and a bible in the other.

Did You Know?

Valverde invited Atahualpa to come down off his litter and share a meal with Francisco Pizarro in private. Atahualpa declined and told Valverde he would not move until the Spanish returned everything they had stolen since their arrival in his kingdom.

Then, Valverde explained his role as a member of the Catholic Church, and handed Atahualpa his bible. Since the Inca had no system of written language, a book was something Atahualpa had never seen before. After looking at the writing inside, which had no meaning to him, Atahualpa tossed the bible onto the ground. Valverde, shocked and angered by Atahualpa's disrespect for God and the Catholic religion, gave the signal to attack.

Two cannons were fired into the enormous crowd gathered in the square. As the smoke began to spread, soldiers on horseback burst out from the buildings and began wildly attacking. The Inca soldiers panicked and in trying to retreat through the one small opening in the plaza, trampled each other to death.

Atahualpa was captured and as many as 5,000 Inca died in the fight. Not one Spaniard was killed.

To the Inca people, the Sapa Inca was a god, a descendant of the sun. To see him captured by such a small group of people was devastating. How could a god be defeated? With its leader captured, the Inca Empire was left in a state of shock and disbelief.

Promises Made, Promises Broken

Atahualpa noticed that Pizarro and his men were obsessed with gold and silver. In return for his freedom, Atahualpa promised to fill a room 17 feet wide (5 meters), 22 feet long (7 meters), and 8 feet high (2½ meters) three times—once with items made of gold, and two more times with items made of silver. Atahualpa would have all of these riches delivered from around the Inca Empire in just two months!

Francisco Pizarro and his men were feeling nervous about their situation. They were still outnumbered 500 to one by the Inca, and they were hundreds of miles away from their ships. Was Atahualpa secretly plotting to have one of his armies come and kill them? They pressed Atahualpa to speed up the deliveries of gold and silver.

Trying to calm the Spanish, Atahualpa arranged for some of the conquistadors to be carried on litters (like Inca nobility) to view the huge amounts of treasure in Cuzco.

Other Spanish scouts rode to the coastal city of Pachacamac, the site of an elaborate temple. The men who visited Cuzco returned with 285 llama-loads of gold and silver! But the men who rode to Pachacamac came back empty-handed. The priests of the temple there were on bad terms with Atahualpa and had hidden the gold when they heard the Spanish were coming.

A disagreement broke out over what should be done with Atahualpa. Some Spaniards wanted him put to death for lying about the amount of treasure in his kingdom, while others thought he was more valuable alive. In the end, Atahualpa was killed on July 26, 1533.

The End of the Inca Empire

The Spanish sent for reinforcements, and the two sides fought many battles, some won by the Inca and some won by the Spanish. The Spanish overcame terrible odds to defeat the Inca over and over again. But there were also battles of Spanish against Spanish and Inca against Inca. Pizarro himself was **assassinated** by followers of his partner, Diego de Almagro, exactly eight years to the day after the death of Atahualpa.

WORDS TO KNOW

assassinate: to kill a leader.

execution: carrying out the death sentence of a person found guilty of a crime.

The Inca did not go down easily. Tupac Amaru was the final Sapa Inca descended from royal lineage. His royal complex was built in Vilcabamba, deep in the dense forests where he oversaw the few hundred soldiers left of the once mighty Inca army. It took the Spanish years to find Vilcabamba, but once they did, they easily captured it and Tupac Amaru. Hoping to put an end to native uprisings once and for all, the Spanish staged the **execution** of Tupac Amaru in the central plaza of Cuzco for all to see. When Tupac Amaru was beheaded with a single swing from the executioner's sword, it was clear that the Spanish had conquered the Inca.

CALCULATE THE WEIGHT AND WORTH OF
ATAHUALPA'S RANSOM

The treasure that Atahualpa promised the Spanish was unimaginably huge. Learn how to calculate the capacity of the treasure room and how much the treasure would be worth today.

→ SUPPLIES ←

- pencil
- paper
- calculator
- Internet access

1 Using the formula for the volume of a rectangular prism (length x width x height), you will need to calculate the size of the ransom room. The room measured 17 feet wide (5 meters) by 22 feet long (7 meters), by 8 feet high (2½ meters).

Ransom Room

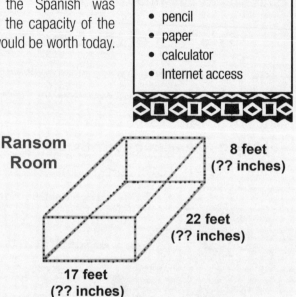

8 feet
(?? inches)

22 feet
(?? inches)

17 feet
(?? inches)

2 How many gold bars would fit in the room in Cajamarca? A standard gold bar measures 8 inches long (20 centimeters) by 3 inches wide (7½ centimeters) by 2 inches high (5 centimeters).

Gold Bar

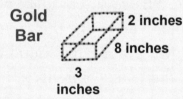

2 inches

8 inches

3 inches

3 How can you figure out how many gold bars—measured in inches (centimeters)—will fit in a room measured in feet (meters)? You need to choose a common unit of measure and convert all of your numbers to that length before you begin. For example, how many inches are in 17 feet?

4 Now calculate the value of these gold bars. Each gold bar weighs 400 ounces. The value of an ounce of gold is constantly changing. You'll need to look up the current value on the Internet or in the newspaper.

5 Can you calculate the value of the silver portion of the ransom? What numbers will you need to find in order to do your calculations?

DOCUMENT

THE SPANISH CONQUEST

The Inca had no written records of their daily lives. They did not write, or use books the way Europeans of the time did. It's quite possible that this caused Atahualpa to throw the bible to the ground and spark the war that would eventually destroy the Inca Empire. In this activity, you will make a book from a single piece of paper. Your book will have a front cover, four pages, and a back cover. Use it to tell the story of the Spanish Conquest in pictures and words.

→ SUPPLIES ←

- sheet of paper
- scissors
- colored pencils

1 Fold the piece of paper in half, then in half again. Fold the paper in half once more, but make a crease only partway up the edge.

2 Open up the last two folds. Cut from the first fold up to the crease you just made. Open the paper up all the way and stand it up with the opening, as shown, like a diamond.

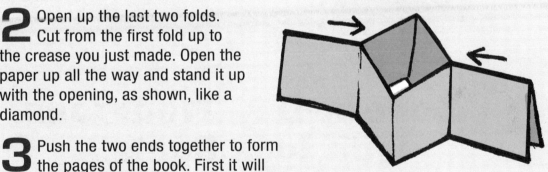

3 Push the two ends together to form the pages of the book. First it will be like the letter *t*. Fold the pages all in one direction. Line up the pages and firmly crease them.

4 Tell your story! Make sure to use pictures as well as words.

CHAPTER 8

☀ Modern-Day Traditions with Inca Roots

The Spanish were determined to defeat the Inca. Against impossible odds the conquistadors occupied their land, stole their riches, and enslaved their people. They also tried to erase the Inca's religious and cultural practices because they were seen as insults to Christianity and the Catholic Church. In the end, the Spanish won, but many Inca customs, traditions, and attitudes survived and live on today.

In the mountains of South America today, the cultural flavors of the region are **vibrant** and **distinctive**. Tourism is a main source of **income** for the region, so customs that were discouraged or even outlawed by the Spanish are being revived and celebrated as attractions for visitors.

Almost every aspect of Andean life has been shaped in some way by the cultures that have lived there for thousands of years.

WORDS TO KNOW

vibrant: full of energy and enthusiasm.

distinctive: an aspect of something that makes it stand out as special or unique.

income: money received for work.

spirituality: a person's system of beliefs about the human spirit or soul.

Festivals and Holidays

When the Spanish came to South America, the indigenous people already had their own concepts of God and **spirituality**. The Spanish tried to force their Catholic religion on the local population, but it didn't work. What happened instead was that elements of Spanish Catholicism combined with important aspects of Inca mythology to create a unique blend of religion.

The festival of Corpus Christi in Cuzco takes place every year in June, 60 days after Easter. Hundreds of groups dance to music that is a mix of European marches and Andean melodies.

Dancing groups practice for months before the celebration and wear elaborate costumes as they dance through the city streets for miles.

The culmination of the festival is the procession of the saints. Fifteen enormous sculptures of Catholic saints are carefully carved and decorated. Then, as the Inca once carried their kings, church members carry these sculptures on litters around the city of Cuzco. Some of the sculptures weigh more than 1,000 pounds (450 kilograms) and are lugged around for hours!

Ritual Battle

In some rural regions of the Andes, a ritual battle called a Tinku (tin-koo) still takes place. This competition between communities involves music, dancing, and fighting. Competitors march from their villages into the main plaza of a central town. The Tinku fighters wear bright, intricately woven clothing and helmets made of hardened leather. Two fighters square off and begin their match by swaying back and forth in unison in a simple dance until one throws the first punch. Then the fight is on and it ends when one of the fighters is knocked off his feet. This ancient ritual has become a tourist attraction and has even appeared on television and in magazines all over the world. The government and modern-day police tolerate Tinku fights but quickly put an end to them if they get too violent.

Occurring a few weeks after the festival of Corpus Christi, residents of Cuzco organize an Inti Raymi celebration. The fountain in the main plaza in Cuzco is covered in painted plywood and turned into a stage resembling a giant rock formation.

> *Hundreds of actors in traditional dress from the various regions of the historical Inca Empire walk in a formal procession from the city center up to the ruins of Saqsaywaman.*

Did You Know?

Many of the dancers in Cuzco's religious parades wear amazing masks. Some depict the angry faces of white men with curled mustaches and long noses. These masks represent the faces of the conquistadors who beat and enslaved the indigenous people, and wearing them is a way for the Andean people to both recognize and make fun of them.

In the field at the center of Saqsaywaman, an actor playing the role of the Sapa Inca carries out rituals that people imagine the Inca may have performed. The re-creation of the Inti Raymi is so popular that the hills surrounding the ceremony are covered with tens of thousands of spectators. A mix of locals and tourists watch as the ancient rites are acted out.

Clothing and Styles

On paved streets between modern skyscrapers in La Paz, Bolivia, you will find *campesinas* (comp-ay-see-nahs) dressed in embroidered shirts, pleated skirts, bowler hats, and braids. These country women are often carrying children or supplies in a woven blanket tied around their shoulders.

> **Campesinas *live with one foot in the modern world and one foot in the past.***

Neatly braided hair and use of the *lliqlla* blankets are traditions that go back thousands of years. But it wasn't until the early 1900s that *campesinas* in the cities started wearing bowler hats and pleated skirts. The unique styles of the Andean people reflect a mixture of influences from far away with traditions and practices that have existed for centuries.

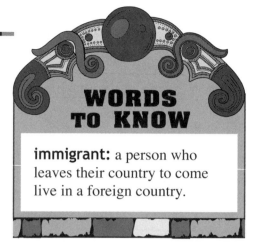

WORDS TO KNOW

immigrant: a person who leaves their country to come live in a foreign country.

Bowler Hats

The bowler hat style of the Aymara women of Peru and Bolivia may have gotten its start, at least in part, by accident. Thomas and William Bowler designed the hats in 1849 for English gentlemen to wear horseback riding. How did they end up in South America? One story says they were sent to European **immigrants** who were building railroads through South America. The hats were too small for their heads so they gave them to the indigenous people to use. Another story says that the manufacturer made too many hats and sold them to the people of the Andes. In either case, the hats are not very practical—they aren't warm, they are too small to fit properly on one's head, and they don't offer protection from the sun or rain. But they have become a distinctive fixture in the style of the women of the high Andes.

Industry

The Inca were highly skilled in large-scale farming, working with precious metals, and textile art.

Not surprisingly, these three areas are important industries today in Peru, Bolivia, and Ecuador.

Mining: The land that once belonged to the Inca is rich with valuable mineral deposits. Enormous mining operations for gold, silver, and tin exist throughout the region. In the Bolivian city of Potosí, an entire mountain has been riddled with holes and tunnels. It is called El Cerro Rico (el sair-oh reek-oh), which means the Mountain of Riches. Almost all the silver the Spanish took from South America came from this one mountain!

Locked underneath the Salar de Uyuni, a dry salt lake in central Bolivia, is the highest concentration of **lithium** on the planet. Some experts believe this is a valuable resource that could bring wealth to the region in the near future. With more and more manufacturers looking for ways to make goods that use less energy and fewer resources, lithium will be in high demand.

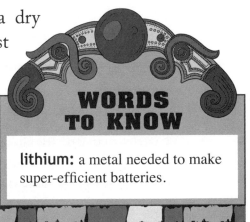

WORDS TO KNOW

lithium: a metal needed to make super-efficient batteries.

Did You Know?

Deep inside almost every Andean mine is a sculpture of a life-size devil known as El Tío (el tee-oh). It sits alone in a dark chamber. Miners, almost all of whom are indigenous men, pay tribute to El Tío by giving him cigarettes, beer, and coca leaves. They hope that offering these goods to the god of the underworld will protect them from the many dangers of working underground in mines.

Textiles: Another valuable South American resource is the fine wool of the alpaca. The high Andes is the only place in the world where alpacas are naturally found, and vast herds of them are tended from Peru to Argentina. Much of their wool is sent to cities like Arequipa, Peru, where machines process it into luxurious fabrics and threads. Textiles and clothes made of alpaca are among the most expensive in the world.

Fruits and Vegetables: The combination of fertile soil, bright sun, and ample water made the Andes an ideal place for the Inca to grow food and build their empire. These same conditions exist today, and thanks to advances in technology, more food can now be grown on the land.

WORDS TO KNOW

export: something sent to be sold in other countries.

commerce: buying and selling things.

Maybe your dinner includes something grown in Peru. Believe it or not, on any given day, a plane flying to a foreign country from Peru might carry as much weight in fresh fruit and vegetables as in people! Avocados and asparagus are major **exports** from the Andes to countries in North America and Europe. As a result of this **commerce**, some communities have become quite successful.

But there is a downside. Growing enough food for a local population, like the people of the Inca Empire, and using water from rivers and lakes, was a **sustainable** use of the land. But when crops are grown for cash instead of **subsistence**, people try to grow as much as possible to make as much money as they can. This forces farmers to take water from **aquifers**—underground water sources.

Today the aquifers are beginning to dry up. If South American farmers use too much of the water, in the future they may not be able to grow enough crops to feed the people in their own countries.

WORDS TO KNOW

sustainable: when resources are used in a way that does not use them up.

subsistence: making or growing things to support oneself only, not to sell them.

aquifer: a section of rock underground that contains water.

produce: fresh fruits and vegetables.

Eating Local Food

Buying fruits and vegetables that are shipped to your store from far away has hidden costs. It takes a lot of energy to move **produce** great distances. Since fruits and vegetables spoil quickly, they have to be moved fast or be refrigerated. Trucks and airplanes are the most common modes of transportation, and the price you pay at the grocery store has the cost of using this transportation built into it. But trucks and airplanes burn fuel that pollutes the air. If you are in the United States and you take a bite out of an apple that was grown in Chile, you are eating something that took a lot more energy to arrive at your mouth than an apple grown at a local orchard. Eating foods that are raised or grown locally was the way of the Inca. If we all do the same, our food will be cheaper, fresher, and better for our planet and for us!

MAKE YOUR OWN
DEVIL MASK

A popular mask during the dances of Corpus Christi and Carnaval in Peru is a simple stocking cap embroidered to look like a devil. You can make something similar using a paper plate and some markers. When you are done, go dance around the neighborhood and see what your friends say!

1 Hold the paper plate up to your face and gently fold it around your head. Using the scissors, trim off the sides of the plate so it has the same shape as your face.

2 Hold the trimmed plate over your face and locate the spots where your eyes are. Have a friend make a mark on these spots with a pencil.

3 Take the mask off your face and carefully cut out the holes for your eyes.

4 Using the illustration provided as a guide, draw a mustache, eyebrows, and a beard on the plate. Get creative with colors!

5 Punch a hole on either side of the mask. Tie the string or elastic on.

6 Wearing a hat with a brim or a stocking cap will make the devil mask look even more authentic and creepy!

LEARN TO BRAID

The tradition of braiding hair is a custom that was important to the Inca, and also to many of the cultures that came before them. In modern-day South America, almost all rural Andean women wear their hair in two neat braids. Practice making a single braid with a friend's hair or some yarn. Once you have got it down, see if you can create two side-by-side braids in the Andean style.

1 Gently brush any tangles out of the hair you are going to braid. Sometimes spraying the hair with water or detangler can help.

2 Divide the hair into three separate parts, left, right, and middle.

3 Take the strand on the left. Pass it over the middle strand and under the right strand.

4 Take the strand that is now on the left and pass it over the middle and under the right.

5 Continue this pattern until you have braided almost the full length of hair.

6 Secure the end of the braid with an elastic or with a piece of colorful yarn.

7 To make two braids, first part the hair right down the middle, from the forehead all the way over the head to the neck. Then follow the directions above for each side of the braid.

WHERE DOES YOUR FOOD COME FROM?

The Inca grew food to feed their empire, but the way they did it was both efficient and clever. They learned to preserve food by drying it. This made it lighter to carry and also allowed it to sit for long periods of time without spoiling. In today's global economy, fresh food is flown by airplane all over the world. This "long-distance farming" has an impact on both the price of the food and the health of our planet. You might be surprised at how well traveled your food is!

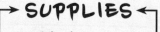

1 As you buy food over the next few months, look at the labels on the fruits and vegetables. Where were they grown? Keep a list of the specific foods and the states and countries it came from.

3 Do a taste test! Can you buy a local apple and an apple grown far away? Which tastes better? See how many different types of food you can test this way.

2 Put your map up on a wall that you can make holes in. Look at your list and use pushpins to mark all of these locations on a map. Where does most of your food come from? What is the farthest your food travels?

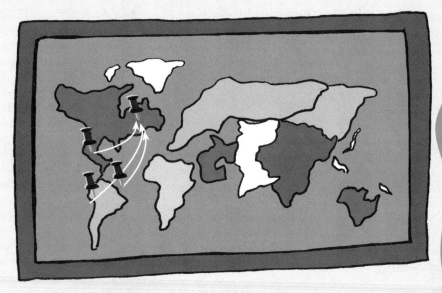

GLOSSARY

abstract: existing more in thought and ideas than in reality.

acute angle: an angle smaller than 90 degrees.

adaptation: a change that a living thing makes to become better suited to its environment.

adapt: to change to survive in new or different conditions.

administration: a system to manage a large group of people, such as a city or country.

adobe: a building material made of sun-dried clay and straw, commonly used in areas of little rainfall.

agricultural terracing: reshaping sloping land into a series of steps.

agriculture: growing crops and raising animals for food.

alpine: describing the high mountains.

alpine cirque: a bowl-shaped mountain valley.

altar: a raised area where religious ceremonies are performed.

altiplano: the high flat land surrounding Lake Titicaca.

altitude: the height above the level of the sea. Also called elevation.

Amazon basin: the land area in central and eastern South America that the water flows across or under to reach the Amazon River.

ambush: a sneak attack.

Andean: relating to the Andes Mountains.

Andes Mountains: the mountain range that runs the length of western South America. It is the world's longest mountain range above sea level.

appease: to please someone by giving in to their demands.

aquifer: a section of rock underground that contains water.

archaeologist: a scientist who studies people through the objects they left behind.

artifact: an object made by people in the past, including tools, pottery, and jewelry.

assassinate: to kill a leader.

assimilate: to absorb a person or group into a larger group.

astronomical event: something that happens because of the movement of the sun, moon, or stars.

astronomy: the movement of the sun, moon, and stars.

atmosphere: the gases that surround the earth.

barren: bare land with poor soil and few plants.

bureaucrat: someone who helps run a government.

buttress: a support in a building that projects out from a wall.

cache: a collection of things in a place that is hidden or secured.

canyon: a deep, narrow valley with steep sides.

carbohydrate: a chemical compound in foods that contains sugar and starch.

cardinal directions: the main points on a compass—north, south, east, and west.

Catholic Friar: a man employed by the Catholic Church.

centralize: to bring together in one place.

CE: put after a date, CE stands for Common Era. It counts up from zero to the present year.

ceremonial: using ceremonies to celebrate special events.

characteristic: a feature of a person, place, or thing.

chicha: a beer made from corn.

civic: relating to duty and responsibility to community.

civilization: a community of people that is advanced in art, science, and government.

113

mortar: a clay-like substance used to connect blocks or bricks to each other. Mortar is wet when first mixed, but dries hard.

mourning: grieving after death.

mummy: a dead body that has been preserved so that it doesn't decay.

mythology: a set of stories or beliefs about a particular religion or culture.

navigable: large enough for boats and ships to travel on.

New World: North and South America.

niche: a shallow recess in a wall.

nobility: considered the most important people in a society.

Northern Hemisphere: the half of the earth north of the equator.

nutrient: substances in food and soil that living things need to live and grow.

obtuse angle: an angle greater than 90 degrees.

ornamental: decorative.

ornate: decorated intricately, with complex patterns and shapes.

oxbow: a U-shaped bend in a river.

peak: the pointed top of a mountain.

pictorial: something expressed in pictures or art.

pilgrimage: a journey to a place that is spiritually important.

plateau: a large, raised area of land that is fairly flat and often cut by deep canyons.

plumb bob: a weight suspended from a string that creates a line perfectly perpendicular to the horizon.

politician: someone who is part of the government.

precipitation: falling moisture in the form of rain, sleet, snow, or hail.

precision: accuracy.

pre-Columbian: the time before Christopher Columbus came to the New World.

predecessors: people who came before.

preserve: to save food in a way that it won't spoil.

produce: fresh fruits and vegetables.

puna: a high, flat area in the Andes.

quarried: dug from an open pit.

Quechua: the language of the Inca, created to communicate with hundreds of different groups of people.

ration: a fixed amount.

reign: the period of time a ruler rules.

relic: an object that is important because of its age or connection with the past.

remnant: a small remaining amount of something.

representation: a depiction of things in pictures or other forms of art.

resources: something used by people to help them take care of themselves.

retreat: to withdraw from something threatening.

ridge: a long, narrow high area of land, usually linking together mountains or hills.

right angle: an angle that measures exactly 90 degrees, like at the corner of a square or rectangle.

rite of passage: a ceremony marking an important stage in a person's life.

ritual: something done as part of a religion.

royalty: members of a ruling class of people.

sacrifice: the killing of a person or animal as an offering to a god.

saturated: to be full of water.

scale: the size of something.

scholar: someone who has done advanced study of a subject.

seismic: relating to earthquakes.

shrine: a special, religious place.

silo: a tower used to store grain.

soil: the top layer of the earth.

solstice: the day around June 21 and December 21 when the day is either shortest or longest depending on whether you are north or south of the equator.

Southern Hemisphere: the half of the earth south of the equator.

spiritual: religious; relating to the soul or spirit.

spirituality: a person's system of beliefs about the human spirit or soul.

stable: regular and predictable.

stimulant: a substance that increases energy levels.

subduction: when one tectonic plate slides beneath another.

subsistence: making or growing things to support oneself only, not to sell them.

summer solstice: the day of the year with the greatest amount of sunlight.

suppressant: something that prevents an event from happening.

surplus: an amount of something that is left over after normal demands have been met.

sustainable: when resources are used in a way that does not use them up.

symbolic: something that is important because of what it stands for or represents.

symmetrical: the same on all sides.

tectonic plate: a large slab of the earth's crust that is in constant motion. It moves on the hot, melted layer of earth below.

terrace: an area of flat land carved into a hillside, often used for farming.

textiles: cloth or fabric.

topography: the shape of the landscape.

torrential rain: very heavy rain.

trapezoid: a four-sided shape with two parallel sides.

tribute: a gift or act intended to show respect, gratitude, or admiration.

tunic: a loose shirt made without sleeves worn by men in many ancient cultures.

urban: relating to cities or towns.

valley: a long, low area between hills or mountains, often following a river or stream.

vibrant: full of energy and enthusiasm.

vicuñas and guanacos: small Andean hoofed animals related to the camel with coats of very fine wool.

viscacha: an Andean rodent with very fine fur that looks like a rabbit. Related to the llama and alpaca.

volcano: an opening in the earth's surface through which melted rock, ash, and gases erupt.

water vapor: water as a gas, like steam or mist.

weathering: destruction from rain, snow, wind, and sun.

weather: temperature, cloudiness, rainfall, and wind.

winter solstice: the day of the year with the least amount of sunlight.

yield: the amount of a crop harvested on an area of land.

RESOURCES

Books

Bernand, C. *The Incas: Empire of blood and gold.*
London: Thames and Hudson, 1994.

D'Altroy, T. N. *The Incas.* Oxford: Blackwell, 2003.

Elorrieta, S. F., & Elorrieta, S. E. *Cusco and the sacred valley of the Incas.*
Cusco, Perú: Tanpu S.R.L, 2003.

Frost, P. *Exploring Cusco.* Lima, Peru: Nuevas Imágenes, 1999.

Helfer, A. J. *Discovering Machu Picchu: The Inca trail and Choquequirau : The essential book.* Catalina, Lima [Peru: Ediciones Del Hipocampo, 2004.]

Hemming, J. *The conquest of the Incas.*
New York: Harcourt, Brace, Jovanovich, 1970.

Julien, C. J. *Reading Inca history.* Iowa City: University of Iowa Press. 2000.

Moseley, M. E. *The Incas and their ancestors: The archaeology of Peru.*
London: Thames & Hudson, 2001.

Silverblatt, I. *Moon, sun, and witches: Gender ideologies and class in Inca and colonial Peru.* Princeton, NJ: Princeton University Press, 1987.

Stone, R. *Art of the Andes: From Chavín to Inca.*
London: Thames & Hudson, 2002.

Websites

The Incas for Kids: **www.incas.mrdonn.org/roads.html**

Inca Religion: **www.philtar.ac.uk/encyclopedia/latam/inca.html**

Peru: Inca Bridge Photo Album: **www.rutahsa.com/k-chaca.html**

History of the Inca:
www.historyworld.net/wrldhis/PlainTextHistories.asp?historyid=ac84

NOVA Ice Mummies of the Inca:
www.pbs.org/wgbh/nova/ancient/ice-mummies-inca.html

Inca Architecture: **www.rutahsa.com/incaarch.html**

Agricultural Terraces and Irrigation Canals; The Cusichaca Trust:
www.cusichaca.org/page20.htm

Textiles de Bolivia: **www.home.schule.at/teacher/evelinerochatorrez/spanisch/textiles_potosinos.htm**

Inca History: **www.historyworld.net**

INDEX

PUBLISHED BY THE PRESS SYNDICATE OF THE UNIVERSITY OF CAMBRIDGE
The Pitt Building, Trumpington Street, Cambridge CB2 1RP, United Kingdom

CAMBRIDGE UNIVERSITY PRESS
The Edinburgh Building, Cambridge CB2 2RU, United Kingdom
40 West 20th Street, New York, NY 10011-4211, USA
10 Stamford Road, Oakleigh, Melbourne 3166, Australia

First published 1997

Printed in the United Kingdom at the University Press, Cambridge
Designed and produced by Gecko Limited, Bicester, Oxon.

Typeset in Times Roman

A catalogue record for this book is available from the British Library

ISBN 0 521 46601 6   paperback

Acknowledgements
The publisher would like to thank Christine Kinealy and Carmel Gallagher for their contributions
to the writing of this book.

Illustrations by: Gecko Limited, Martin Sanders and Sam Thompson

Cover: *Background* The known world in 1457 (Genoese World Map) by permission of the
Syndics of Cambridge University Library
Main picture An illustration from a 14th-century French manuscript showing Thomas Despenser,
Earl of Gloucester, meeting Art MacMurrough Kavanagh, King of Leinster, in 1399, reproduced
by courtesy of the Trustees of the British Library

Picture research by: Sandie Huskinson-Rolfe of PHOTOSEEKERS
Aerofilms of Borehamwood: pp. 27, 28; Ancient Art and Architecture Collection: pp. 8, 31*tr*; British
Library, London/Bridgeman Art Library, London (Roy 15E IV f.236, Coronation of William I, Anciennes
Chroniques d'Angleterre, 15 century): p. 16, (Cott Claud DII f.33, William the Conqueror, Liber Legum
Antiquorum Regum, c.1321): p. 18, (Add 42130 f.73, Luttrell Psalter, 14 century): p. 31*m*, (Add 42130
f.68, Luttrell Psalter, 14 century): p. 31*cr*, (Cott Tib B.V. f.5, Peasants tending sheep, Anglo-Saxon
Miscellany, c.1030): p. 35*tl*, (Cott Tib B.V. f.8, Warming and Smithying, Anglo-Saxon Misc., c.1030):
p. 35*cr*, (Cott Tib B.V. Part 1 f.5v, Hay Making and Ploughing, Anglo-Saxon Misc., c.1030): p. 35*bl*, (Roy
10E IV f.187, Nun and monk in stocks, Smithfield Decretals, c.1330–40): p. 41, (Harl 5102 f.32, Murder
of Thomas a Becket, 13 century): p. 43, National Library of Scotland, Edinburgh/Bridgeman (f.7, Robert
the Bruce and his wife, 1306, Seton's Armorial Crests): p. 23, Trinity College, Cambridge/Bridgeman
(Ms R 17 I f.283v, Monk Eadwine, Eadwine Psalter, c.1150): p. 40; By permission of the British Library
(Ms Ar. 91 f.218v): p. 31*cl*, (Ms Roy 2.B.VII f.15): p. 31*bl*, (Ms Sloane 2435 f.85, The Cleric..): p. 42;
Courtesy of Dublinia Limited: pp. 37, 61; Edinburgh Photographic Library/David Morrison: p. 59;
ET Archive: p. 48; Chris Fairclough Colour Library: p. 63*tl*; Sonia Halliday & Laura Lushington: p. 21;
Robert Harding Picture Library/Philip Craven: p. 19; Michael Holford: pp. 9*l&r*, 10, 15, 32, 38; Irish
Tourist Board/Brian Lynch: p. 63*b*; Lensmen Associates: p. 63*tr*; The Mansell Collection: p. 39; National
Gallery of Ireland: p. 51; National Library of Ireland, from Guizot's l'Histoire de France, p. 50, NLI: p. 58;
Public Record Office Image Library: p.20*l&r*; The Slide File: pp. 57*l&r*, 62*l&r*; Photograph reproduced
with kind permission of the Trustees of the Ulster Museum, Belfast, © Robert McKelvey: p. 56.

CONTENTS

Section 1:
The Norman Conquest

Section 2:
Aspects of medieval society

Section 3:
The Normans in Ireland

The conquest of Britain

1 The Normans

The first Normans were Viking pirates who settled on the north coast of France. The French called them 'Northmen' and, in AD 911, the king of France granted them land which became known as Normandy. The Normans were fierce fighters and soon conquered many parts of Europe and the Middle East in the search for more land.

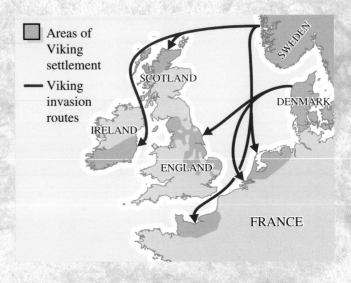

2 Contenders for the throne of England

In 1066 the English king, Edward the Confessor, died. There were three contenders for his throne: Harold of Wessex; William, Duke of Normandy; and Harald Hardraada, King of Norway. The king's council was called the Witan and they decided to make Harold of Wessex the next king of England. This angered the others, each of whom claimed that the throne rightfully belonged to him.

3 The fight for the throne, 1066

During the year 1066, Harold, the newly appointed king, had to fight to keep his crown. Harald of Norway invaded England, landing in the north, but was defeated by King Harold's army at the Battle of Stamford Bridge. King Harold's army then marched to the south coast to fight a second invasion force led by William of Normandy. This time King Harold's army was defeated and he himself was killed at the Battle of Hastings.

4 The Norman Conquest after 1066

William of Normandy became the new king in 1066 and set out to bring all of England under his control. He used terror to put down any rebel English lords and built castles to control the countryside. William introduced the feudal system, which divided the conquered lands between the king, the Church and the Norman barons and knights. To find out about his new kingdom, William organised the Domesday survey, which listed in detail the conditions in the kingdom, village by village.

5 William the Conqueror

Different pieces of evidence about William of Normandy give us conflicting impressions of him. Some writers say he was ruthless and cruel. Others say he was clever and quite a religious man who was a good leader and a careful organiser. William died in France in 1087.

6 The Normans in Wales and Scotland

Twenty years after the invasion of 1066, the Normans had conquered most of England, but it was to be almost 200 years before Wales was completely under their control. Norman lords built huge castles along the border with Wales to prevent attacks from Welsh rebels. In Scotland only some parts of the country came under Norman control and the rest remained in the power of Scottish lords.

1

The Normans

The Normans are thought to have descended from Viking pirates who came from the north of Europe and gradually moved south, conquering different lands and sometimes settling in them. By AD 1000, the Normans had gained control of a whole province in northern France which became known as Normandy. In 1066 the Normans conquered England, and their leader, William of Normandy, became king of England.

Why were the Normans so successful in conquering other lands?

About AD 911, Charles the Simple, King of France, gave some land in his country to the 'Northmen', who were Viking raiders. It was known as 'Northmannia' or 'Normandy'. The leader of the Northmen was Rollo. In return for this land, his soldiers fought for King Charles. The Northmen had been pagans but, after they were given Normandy, they became Christians. They also began to speak French and, because of this, many people referred to them as Frenchmen.

The Normans were fierce and brave soldiers. Even after they had settled in Normandy they still conquered new lands. Sometimes they did this quickly, sometimes it took many years. The most famous of all the Norman conquests was England, conquered in 1066. Not only was it quick – the battle was over in a day – but it was permanent. William of Normandy became the king of England and the Normans who settled in England became wealthy.

What were the Normans like?

Many of the descriptions which survive about the Normans were written after the Norman Conquest of England. The following sources give two views of the Normans.

Source A

The Normans are careful about how they dress and what they eat. They are a race used to war and can hardly live without it. They are faithful to their lords but will betray them if upset. They are the most polite of people and even marry their subjects. After they came to England they supported the Church. You can see churches in every village, but they build monasteries in towns and cities.

William of Malmesbury, an English monk writing in about 1125

Source B

Why should we worry about victory, when God himself has made victory the right of our people? We ourselves won England in only a short time and have brought our own laws. Who was it if not men of our Norman race, who conquered Apulia, Calabria and Sicily?

Walter Espec, a Norman baron, writing in about 1138

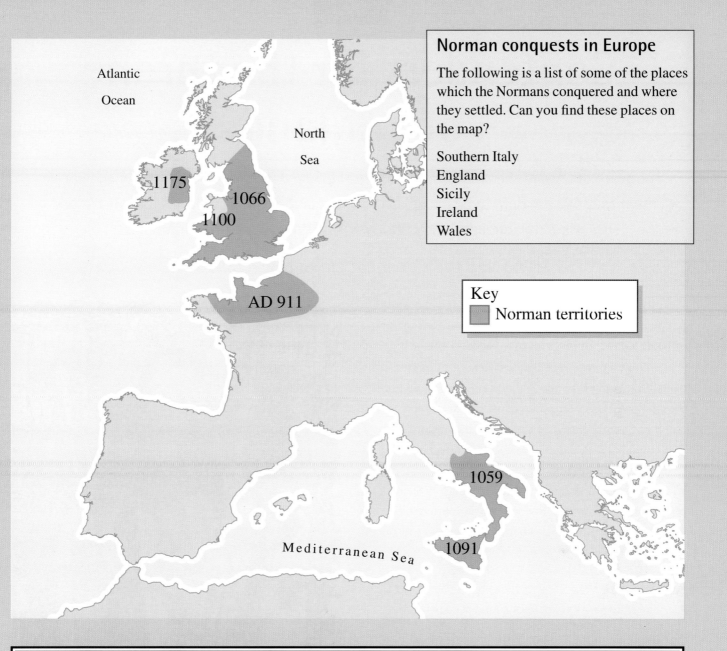

Atlantic
Ocean

North
Sea

1175

1066

1100

AD 911

Mediterranean Sea

1059

1091

Norman conquests in Europe

The following is a list of some of the places which the Normans conquered and where they settled. Can you find these places on the map?

Southern Italy
England
Sicily
Ireland
Wales

Key
▨ Norman territories

1 What do Sources A and B tell you about the Normans' attitudes to:
● war;
● the Church;
● conquering new lands?

2 a Copy the grid. Tick the correct boxes to show which sources contain information on these topics.
b Which source of information did you find most useful? Why?

Information	Maps	Source A	Source B
The Normans' approach and attitude to war			
The Normans' attitude to the Church			
The Normans' treatment of conquered people			

Contenders for the throne of England

The death of Edward the Confessor, in 1066, left England without a king. Three men believed that they had the right to be the next king of England. They were Harold, Earl of Wessex; Harald Hardraada, King of Norway; and William, Duke of Normandy.

Who had the strongest claim to become king?

From 1042 until 1066 England was ruled by the Anglo-Saxon king, Edward the Confessor. When Edward died in 1066, he did not leave a son to succeed him. A dispute arose over who was to be the next king of England, so a decision was made by the Witan about who should rule the country. The Witan was a council of wise men, which included bishops, archbishops and thanes or lords. They decided that Harold of Wessex should be king. The other two contenders believed that this was the wrong decision and refused to accept it. They each had powerful friends and followers who supported their claim. All three contenders believed that God was on their side.

Source A

A picture of Edward the Confessor, King of England from 1042 to 1066, from a stained-glass window in Winchester Cathedral.

Harold Godwin, Earl of Wessex

- He belonged to one of the most powerful families in England.
- He was the brother-in-law of Edward the Confessor.
- He was English.
- He had the support of the Witan.
- Many English people thought he should be king.
- Harold was crowned king in 1066.

Source B

This picture is from the Bayeux Tapestry. The tapestry is a long embroidered cloth which shows many of the events of 1066. It was probably made for William of Normandy's brother. This picture shows that, on his deathbed, Edward reached out to Harold, apparently to show that he should be the next king.

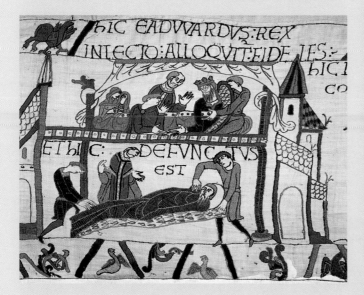

Harald Hardraada, King of Norway

- He claimed to be the rightful heir of King Canute, a Viking who had ruled England.
- He was a great soldier and warrior.
- He was supported by Tostig, Harold's brother.
- He had some support in Viking areas of England.
- He said that Harthacnut, the English king from 1040 to 1042, had promised the English throne to Norway.

William, Duke of Normandy

- William was related to Edward the Confessor.
- The Pope supported William.
- King Edward's mother had been a Norman.
- William claimed that Edward had promised the English crown to him.

Source C

According to the Bayeux Tapestry, Harold had sworn an oath of loyalty to William as the future king of England. Here we see Harold swearing on the bones of saints.

---

1 a Describe what is happening in Sources B and C.
b Which of the sources supports Harold's claim to the throne? How?
c Which of the sources supports William's claim to the throne? How?

2 a Working in groups, look at the claims of Harold of Wessex, Harald Hardraada and William of Normandy. Based on the evidence, different groups should make a case for different contenders to the throne.
b Present each claim to the class. The other groups can ask questions. The class should then discuss:

- How strong are the various claims?
- Which claimants appear to have evidence to support their claims?
- How strong and reliable is the evidence?
- Why was it likely that force would be used to decide the winner?

3

The fight for the throne of England, 1066

In 1066, the Witan chose Harold as King of England. The other contenders to the throne decided not to give up their claims to the throne without a fight.

Who was most likely to be the victor in the struggle for the throne of England?

The crowning of Harold as King of England in 1066 angered both Harald Hardraada of Norway and William, Duke of Normandy. They separately set out to invade England and to claim the throne for themselves. Since early in 1066, William had been making preparations for an invasion, including building a fleet of ships to carry his soldiers to England. William wanted to be ready to invade England before winter, when the English weather made fighting very difficult. Harold was expecting an invasion by William and he kept his army and fleet of ships on the south coast. William's invasion fleet was ready in August but it was prevented from sailing by storms in the Channel. Harold sent part of his army home to harvest their crops. He had to call them back shortly afterwards to face Harald Hardraada of Norway, who had invaded the north of England.

Harold and his army defeated Hardraada and his Norse invaders at the Battle of Stamford Bridge on 25 September. During this battle, Harald Hardraada and his supporter, Earl Tostig, were both killed and the remains of Hardraada's army fled back home to Norway. Harald Hardraada had brought 300 ships to England, but only 24 returned home.

Source A

The crowning of Harold as King of England in 1066, as shown in the Bayeux Tapestry.

No sooner had Harold defeated Harald Hardraada than news reached him that William had landed in Sussex. Harold's army returned at an exhausting pace to confront this new enemy.

Timeline – 1066

18 September	Harald Hardraada and Earl Tostig arrive in England.
25 September	Battle of Stamford Bridge. Harold is the victor. Tostig and Hardraada are killed.
27 September	The Normans sail for England.
28 September	William and his army land in Sussex.
1 October	Harold hears of William's arrival.
13 October	The two armies arrive at Hastings.
14 October	The Battle of Hastings.

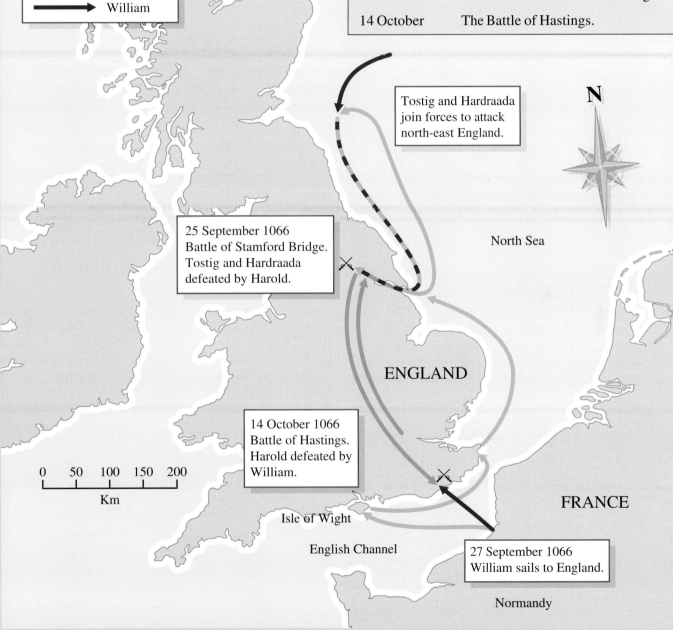

Key
- Hardraada
- Tostig
- Harold
- William

Tostig and Hardraada join forces to attack north-east England.

25 September 1066 Battle of Stamford Bridge. Tostig and Hardraada defeated by Harold.

N

North Sea

ENGLAND

14 October 1066 Battle of Hastings. Harold defeated by William.

Isle of Wight

English Channel

FRANCE

27 September 1066 William sails to England.

Normandy

0 50 100 150 200
Km

This map shows the sites of the major battles in 1066 and the routes taken by the armies.

The Battle of Hastings

Harold took up position at the top of Senlac Hill near Hastings. He placed his best troops, the housecarls, at the front with their shields forming a wall of protection against the Norman arrows. William's knights charged repeatedly up the hill but they could not break through. The Norman archers fired arrows at the shield wall but the housecarls did not break their lines. The battle continued all day until the Normans tricked the English by pretending to run away. The English chased them down the hill, but the Normans turned and attacked again. Harold was killed and the battle was won by William's army.

Contemporary accounts of the battle differ. The following accounts were written at the time of the battle, but by people who were fighting on different sides.

Source B

This account was written by William's priest, who would have had a clear idea of what took place. William may even have confided in him.

Duke William and his men came slowly up the hill, raining death upon the English with their arrows. The English fought back bravely, throwing spears, axes and stones. The Normans were about to retreat when Duke William pushed himself to the front and said 'Look at me. I am still alive and with God's help, I shall be the winner'. With these words, he made the Normans brave again.

Source C

The following is a description of the battle from the *Anglo-Saxon Chronicles*, written by English monks in 1069:

All the English were on foot. The Normans had foot soldiers, archers and cavalry with horses. The battle seemed to go one way and then the other while Harold lived. When the English knew Harold was dead, they began to run away.

Source D

Modern historians know that the Normans were very well organised in battle. In 1994, one wrote:

Historians now recognise that proper recruitment, the use of effective infantry, archery and knights, good leadership and battle planning existed at the time of the Normans.

Sean McGlynn, 'The Myths of Medieval Warfare', in *History Today*, January 1994

---

1 Write a report describing the Battle of Stamford Bridge. Use a computer if possible. Choose the viewpoint of either a supporter of Harold or a supporter of Harald Hardraada. Reports from each side should be read to the class. Discuss how the different viewpoints affect the description of events and the language used.

2 Look at Sources B and C.
a What do they each say is the reason for the victory of the Norman army?
b Why are the two views of the event different?

3 a Explain how each of the following would have helped William to win the Battle of Hastings:
● William's army;
● Harold having just fought another battle;
● mistakes by Harold's men;
● the death of Harold.
b Which do you think is the most important reason?

4 Imagine that newspapers existed at the time of the Battle of Hastings. Working in a group, design and make a front page of a newspaper from 1066, telling of the events in Hastings. It should be from either a Norman or an English viewpoint and can include headlines, articles, cartoons or illustrations. Discuss these reports in the same way that you discussed the Stamford Bridge reports.

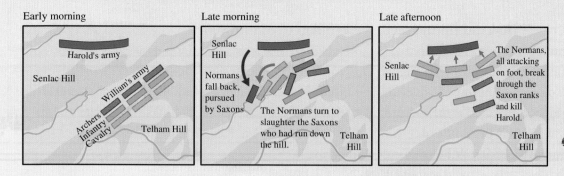

Early morning

Harold's army

Senlac Hill

William's army

Archers
Infantry
Cavalry

Telham Hill

Late morning

Senlac Hill

Normans fall back, pursued by Saxons

The Normans turn to slaughter the Saxons who had run down the hill.

Telham Hill

Late afternoon

Senlac Hill

The Normans, all attacking on foot, break through the Saxon ranks and kill Harold.

Telham Hill

The opposing armies

The two armies each had about 7,000 men but they used different fighting methods.

● *Look at this modern illustration of the Battle of Hastings. Which soldiers do you think are Normans and which are Saxons?*

William the Conqueror

William the Conqueror successfully controlled rebellious nobles and strengthened Normandy against its neighbours. He challenged the authority of the Pope when he married his own cousin, Matilda. In 1066, he invaded and conquered England, which he was soon able to control.

How and why was William successful as a ruler of Normandy and of England?

Once William had won the throne of England he had to keep it. This meant putting down any resistance from the English and keeping control of the Norman knights. There were examples of Normans plundering the newly conquered country and treasures being looted and sent to France. There were a number of challenges to William's authority in the years following the Battle of Hastings but William was able to deal with any threat to his authority in an effective and ruthless manner. Castles were vital to the conquest of England. A programme of castle building was begun to protect William and his Norman supporters from the Anglo-Saxons. They provided bases from which the Normans could control the countryside. William also made new laws to maintain control over his subjects. These included strict forest laws which put the forests under the protection of the king and made hunting illegal without his permission. Punishments could be severe – thieves, for example, could be punished by having their eyes put out.

Source A

This picture, from a medieval manuscript, shows William the Conqueror, riding with his soldiers.

● *What impression of William does this painting give?*

Source B

A statue of William the Conqueror in Falaise in Normandy. William was born in Falaise Castle in late 1027 or early 1028.

Source C

Part of William's death-bed speech, reported by Orderic Vitalis, a twelfth-century Norman monk:

I won a Royal crown, though no ancestor of mine had worn one; it came to me by divine grace, not hereditary right.

Source D

An account by English monks from the _Anglo-Saxon Chronicles_:

The French had possession of the place of slaughter (England), which God granted them because of the nation's sins.

● _What did William claim gave him the right to conquer England? Does Source C agree with William's claim?_

Source E

The 'Harrying of the North' brought criticism even from those who normally praised him:

My narrative has frequently had occasion to praise William, but for this act which condemned the innocent and guilty to die alike by slow starvation I cannot commend him.

The History of Orderic Vitalis

Source F

This is another Saxon description of William's ruthlessness in dealing with the rebels:

Then the outlaws surrendered to him. The king seized ships, weapons, and many treasures, and dealt with his prisoners as he pleased.

The Anglo-Saxon Chronicles

● _How do you think the Anglo-Saxons might have felt about the Norman invaders?_

● _What do Sources D and E tell us about William's treatment of the rebels?_

What did William achieve?

Some historians think that the Normans simply adopted many Anglo-Saxon institutions and laws. There were, however, some clear changes made during William's rule. The Norman system of land ownership, called the 'feudal system', was introduced by William the Conqueror. Latin replaced English as the language for official business and French was spoken at court.

The Domesday Book

William's most lasting achievement was the Domesday Book. This was a detailed survey of England, undertaken very thoroughly by teams of investigators, which told William all about his new country.

Source G

Below A page from the Domesday Book and *(right)* two volumes of the book which was compiled in 1086 on the orders of William the Conqueror.

● *Can you tell what language it is written in?*

The Domesday Book described how many people were living in England, where they lived, what they possessed, what rights they had, and who owned the land. It was a remarkable achievement which still provides valuable information to historians over 900 years after it was written.

● *What does this tell us about William's character? Was he trusting of others?*

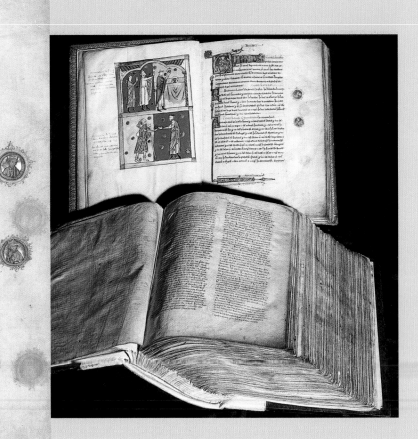

William and the Church

Although William had defied the Pope and married his cousin Matilda, he was keen to show himself to be a good friend of the Church. He built two huge religious houses at Caen, in Normandy, and regained the Pope's favour. The Normans were responsible for introducing grandeur and decoration to church building in England.

William continued to be the Duke of Normandy after he became king of England. He died in 1087 while in France seeing to the defence of Normandy. Before he died he made a gesture of mercy to the people who had suffered from his strict rule. He commanded that all those who were in prison at that time should be set free.

Source I

Though stern beyond measure to those who opposed his will, he was kind to those good men who loved God.

The Anglo-Saxon Chronicles

Source J

He was a harsh man who fought his way into a position of great power. But he was not simply a brutal soldier. His religious changes proved him to be a good man of the Church while the Domesday Book shows his skill as a leader and an organiser.

Robin May, *William the Conqueror and the Normans*, 1984

Source K

The tomb of William the Conqueror in Caen, France.

1 a Which of the following words do you think describe William best: kind, strong, holy, trusting, unholy, good leader, weak, bad leader.
b Select statements from the sources which agree or disagree with the words you have chosen.

2 Write a short essay about William. You can use some of the important points listed below: William's background; his character; important events; his achievements; his legacy.

Life under the Normans

1 Castles

During the early part of the conquest the Normans built temporary wooden forts called motte and bailey castles. These were built to protect the Normans from attack but were also a symbol of their power and control. Eventually many of these castles were rebuilt in stone and became bigger and better protected. The big castles were homes for the wealthy and powerful barons who had received land from the king. In exchange, they had to swear to remain loyal to the king and supply soldiers for his army.

3 Knights, weapons and warfare

The most notable military figure of Norman times was probably the knight on horseback. The knight received land – a village or a manor – from the baron whom he served. Knights trained for years and were skilled fighters who observed a code of conduct known as 'chivalry'. They practised their fighting skills at tournaments, competing against other knights using swords, lances and maces. Archery was encouraged by the king and his lords and most men were expected to practise with

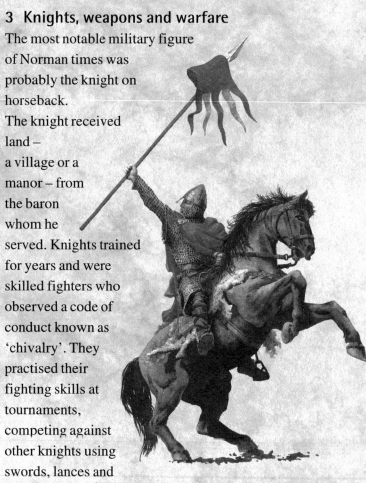

2 The lives of the rich

Living conditions were better for barons and knights than for peasants but life in the castle was still primitive. There were no sewers or running water and rooms could be dirty and cold. The Normans enjoyed large meals with plenty of bread and wine. They introduced a new style of table manners. Dancing was popular at banquets as were jugglers, acrobats and minstrels. Indoor board games were played and hunting was a favourite outdoor pastime.

4 Villages and villeins

Most people worked on the land and lived in small villages or manors. The lord of the manor was a knight whose land was rented out to peasants, called villeins. In return for the use of his land they had to promise to work for him. Each villein had a small strip of land and they shared common land for grazing animals. Their houses were made of wood and their living conditions were very harsh.

5 Towns, craftsmen and merchants

Towns sprang up around the castles but were eventually given a freedom licence or charter. Craftsmen of all kinds worked at their trades and most towns had fairs and markets each week. Villagers came to market to sell farm produce and to buy from the merchants.

6 The Norman Church

The Normans built churches and monasteries all over the country. Like the barons, the bishops received land from the king in exchange for their loyalty and service. Great cathedrals were built to show the power of the Norman lords and bishops. Monasteries were places of learning. Later, friars or priests travelled round the countryside preaching and helping the sick and the poor. Pilgrimages were common in medieval times.

Castles built from wood and stone

We know that castles were important to the success of the Norman conquest of England. The first Norman castles were built quickly as bases for their soldiers. Later some castles also became homes for the lord and his family.

What did these early castles look like?
How did they change throughout the Norman period?

Motte and bailey castles

The Normans usually made their first castles from wood. They were easy and quick to build and there was plenty of timber in the surrounding countryside. Some lords would not allow knights to build stone castles in case they became too powerful.

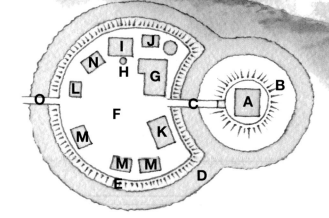

A Wooden tower or keep
B Motte
C Drawbridge from the Motte to the Bailey
D Moated ditch around the Motte and the Bailey
E High fence and fighting platforms around the Bailey

F The Bailey	**K** Hall
G Stables	**L** Weapons store
H Well	**M** Huts for the men to live in
I Cookhouse	**N** Guardroom
J Granary	**O** Outer drawbridge

The main part of the castle was built on a mound of earth which either was an existing hill or had been specially built. This was called a motte. On a lower level was a large courtyard called a bailey. It had sleeping quarters, stables, workshops and storehouses and it was surrounded by a fence. Sometimes, for extra safety, the motte and bailey were separated by a ditch which was dug around the mound and sometimes filled with water. Not all early castles were like this but there is good reason to suppose that most were raised on the motte and bailey plan.

This modern illustration shows what a Norman motte and bailey castle looked like.

Stone castles

The Normans soon replaced the early wooden castles with castles built of stone.
Often, the old wooden defences were rebuilt in stone and the tops of the motte had
stone walls built upon them. They took much longer to build and were built to last.
The remains of many Norman castles are still standing today.

Trebuchet

Siege tower

Mangonel

Stables

Moat

Battlements

Source C

This photograph of Restormel Castle shows how the
stone-built walls replaced earlier wooden fencing.

Moat

Curtain wall

Chapel

Keep

Courtyard

Barbican

Portcullis

Drawbridge

The keep was a square or round tower which was the strongest building inside the castle. It had thick stone walls and narrow windows which were used by archers with bows and arrows. Soldiers were on guard on the battlements on top of the tower, where they could keep a watchful eye on the surrounding countryside. The main entrance into the castle was over a drawbridge. It had the extra protection of a heavy iron gate called a portcullis.

1 Use your library and CD-ROMS to investigate how castles changed in the first hundred years or so after the Norman conquest of England.

2 Explain the advantages of some of the following features of Norman castles:
● the motte;
● the bailey;
● narrow windows;
● the drawbridge;
● the portcullis.

3 Describe the methods used to:
a attack castles;
b defend castles.

4 What difficulties would have faced an attacker of a stone castle?

The lives of the rich

Two extremely important features of Norman England were the castle and the knight. The castle was the key building in the medieval period. It was used to control the land and the people that the Normans had conquered. The lords and knights who lived in the castle, ruled the lives of the people who lived around them.

What was it like to live in a medieval castle?

Living conditions in Norman castles were better than those of the ordinary people who lived outside the castle walls. Even so, life was very basic, especially in terms of cleanliness and sanitation. A lavatory was a shaft in the wall which drained into the moat or a stream. A bath was usually a barrel of water, and it was normal for several people to share the bath water. Rich and poor alike were at risk from widespread disease which was frequently deadly.

Food was very grand and lavish. Medieval banquets were great occasions and sometimes went on for days. The Normans were famed for the amount of wine they would drink. At the table, people were seated according to their status or the favour in which they were held. Less important people had to share bowls. Everyone ate their food from trenchers. These were large, flat pieces of bread, like pizza bases, which were thrown to the dogs after the meal. Etiquette (or rules on how to behave at table) was regarded as being especially important.

Source A

This was written in the thirteenth century in Germany:

A number of people gnaw a bone and then put it back in the dish – this is a serious offence. A man who clears his throat when he eats and one who blows his nose in the table-cloth are ill-bred, I assure you.

First Course

Larded boar's head

Soup made with vegetables

Liver and kidneys flavoured

with blood, vinegar, pepper

and cloves

Various meats

Second Course

Duck, pheasant and chicken

stuffed with egg yolks, currants

and cinnamon

Meat broth

Third Course

Rabbit, hare, woodcock

snipe, pork and cheese pie

Source B

Entertainments

Dancing and feasting were popular in Norman times. Guests at banquets might be entertained by tumblers, jugglers, acrobats, story-tellers, minstrels or musicians and even performing animals, such as the monkey shown below.

Games

On winter evenings indoor games like backgammon, noughts and crosses or draughts were played. Chess was introduced in the tenth century, having been learnt from the Muslims. The rules were simpler than those of today but there were various forms of the game, for example 'The Chase of the Knight' or 'The Battle of the Rooks'.

Hunting

Hunting was a favourite pastime for the Normans. The king set aside forests in England as hunting grounds for the lords he favoured. The Normans introduced rabbits, roe and fallow deer to England. One method of hunting was with trained hawks. Hawks were highly regarded and they were an indication of the status of the lord.

---

1 Look at the menu for the castle banquet.
● What dishes would we still eat?
● What dishes would be unusual today?

2 You are a guest staying at a castle. Using the information in this section write a description of your visit. You should include:
● the conditions in the castle;
● the seating at the table;
● the food;
● the entertainment.

Villages and villeins

After the Norman Conquest of England, William the Conqueror introduced the feudal system, which was a way of dividing land and controlling people. Most people lived and worked on the land which was owned by the lord. From the nobleman at the top to the peasant at the bottom, everyone knew their place.

What was life like in the feudal society?

The feudal system

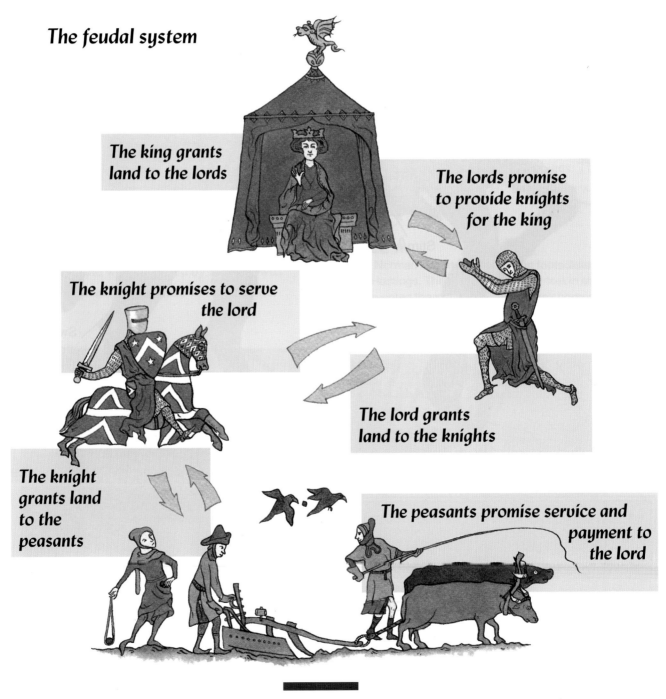

The king grants land to the lords

The lords promise to provide knights for the king

The knight promises to serve the lord

The lord grants land to the knights

The knight grants land to the peasants

The peasants promise service and payment to the lord

Source A

These pictures show different farming activities. How many can you identify? They come from an eleventh-century Anglo-Saxon calendar.

Food was simple and meat was scarce. If people caught rabbits or deer in the royal forest, they were guilty of poaching, for which there were very severe penalties. The simplest houses were shaped like ridge tents and held up by wooden branches. They had roofs of thatch or turf and bare earth floors. Better houses had vertical walls which could be plastered with clay. The poorer people had to use the facilities in the lord's manor because they had none of their own. Corn had to be milled at the lord's mill, bread baked in his oven and metal prepared in his forge. The lord could charge what he chose for the use of his facilities.

The land around the village was divided into two or three very large fields which were laid out in strips and divided up among the population. Around the field there was usually rough grazing land for the animals. There were many woodlands which provided fuel and timber for building.

There was a wide variety of farming activities in the Norman period, particularly cultivating crops such as wheat, rye, barley and oats and tending animals such as sheep and pigs.

Most people were peasants who were allowed to work on the lord's land without paying rent. In exchange they had to do a certain number of days' work for the lord without being paid. They also had to pay a range of taxes and were not allowed to leave the lord's lands. At the very bottom of society were the serfs. They had no land, were extremely poor, were not free and were little more than slaves.

---

1 Make a list of the work done by the peasants who worked on the land.

2 Draw your own diagram to explain how the feudal system worked.

3 How did the feudal system help the Normans keep control of England?

11

Towns, craftsmen and merchants

Today more people live in towns than in the countryside. In medieval England the opposite was true – over 90 per cent of people lived in small country villages.

How did towns develop in the Middle Ages?

In the Middle Ages, towns were small compared to modern towns but in the twelfth century they began to grow in size and in number. As well as developing and extending earlier Saxon towns, the Normans set up towns on new sites, often close to new castles. Towns which were originally built for defensive purposes, later became centres for trade and commerce.

Although most people lived in the countryside, the town was important because it had a market. Many towns were given licences to hold fairs and markets one day a week. This was an opportunity for people from the countryside to come and sell crops and livestock.

Source A

Immediately after the Norman Conquest towns were built as fortresses for the protection of the ruling classes and for the control of newly captured territory. In the twelfth century towns were usually sited to take advantage of the economic rather than the defensive potential of new sites.

Jeremy Haslam, *Early Medieval Towns in Britain,* 1985

This map shows the main towns in England in the fourteenth century.

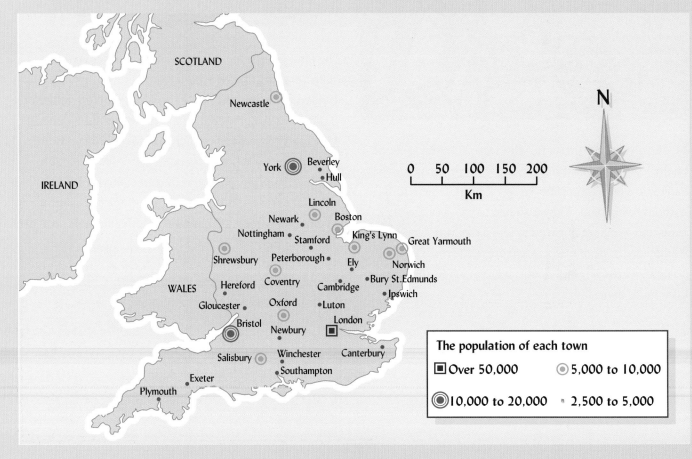

Crafts

The town was also a centre for craftsmen like bakers, masons, butchers, blacksmiths and tanners. A craftsman had to serve an apprenticeship, during which time he learned his craft or trade. Then he could join a guild, which was like a trade union and controlled the quality of the work done by the craftsmen. Different trades could be found in different areas of the town, and streets were often called after the craftsmen who worked there, for example Cook Street, Tailors Lane, Tanners Row.

Merchants

Merchants bought goods and re-sold them at a higher price to make a profit. They exported goods such as corn, wood and hides and imported wine, cloth, salt and spices. People who lived in the towns had little power; like the people in the villages they had to obey the local landowner and the king. As towns became wealthier and traders were able to organise themselves into guilds, townspeople were able to gain some control over their lives. The richer merchants started to meet in the Guildhall to make decisions about how their towns should be run.

Source B

This photograph from the Dublinia exhibition in Dublin shows a reconstruction of a scene from medieval town life. It shows a leather worker sitting outside his place of work. Living conditions in the towns were as poor as those in the countryside. In fact, in some ways they were worse because cramped conditions were an ideal breeding ground for many diseases.

1 Explain why the Normans built towns.

2 What types of goods were bought and sold during market days?

3 Describe how a young man became a craftsman in a medieval town.

4 Imagine that you are a young craftsman who has moved from the countryside to the town. How does your new life compare to your old life?

12

The Norman Church

Between 1066 and 1500 nearly everyone who lived in Britain was a Christian and there was only one Church – the Catholic Church. The Normans built churches and monasteries all over the country. Norman bishops and abbots were given much of the land of England and they supplied the king with soldiers and knights in the same way as the other lords did under the feudal system.

Why was the Church so important? How was it organised?

The Anglo-Saxons were Christians but they did not always obey the Pope. When William invaded England he had the backing of the Pope who hoped that William would bring the English Church under the control of Rome. The Normans built many churches, cathedrals and monasteries over the next century. By 1300 there were 8,000 churches in England. A cathedral was the main church in a diocese where the bishop preached. The Normans saw churches and cathedrals as part of their system of government to control the English.

Source A

A historian's view of cathedrals:

A cathedral is technically the seat (in Latin 'cathedra') of a bishop, however they became much more than just the main church of a diocese. It was sincerely believed that they had to be grand and magnificent to show the power of God. They needed to reflect the glories of heaven, and enable services to be as impressive as possible.

Paul Stollard, writing in *History Today,* February 1993

Source B
Canterbury Cathedral.

The power of the Church

The Church was very powerful for two reasons:

- People were afraid of going to hell when they died, so they obeyed the laws of the Church.
- The Church collected tithes or Church taxes and was very wealthy.

Source C

A bishop describes hell:

> God will sit as a stern judge above all the people. Sinners will suffer great misery as the horrible pit of hell opens up. Large numbers of devils will appear to drag them to the torture and burning of hell.
>
> Anselm, Archbishop of Canterbury, written in the late eleventh century

Church tithes, or taxes, made the clergy unpopular. There were taxes known as 'Mass Pennies' and 'Peter's Pence'. Also, when the head of a household died, his best animal was taken as a tax by the lord of the manor.

Some clergy insisted that the second-best animal should be handed over to the Church.

The church was the centre of village life in medieval times. Announcements were made there and people met there to gossip. The Church controlled many aspects of people's lives. Baptisms and marriages called for short ceremonies; funerals were longer. The funeral of John Paston in Norwich, for example, had 38 priests, 23 nuns and 65 choirmasters in attendance. There was generally a big feast after a funeral. Sundays and Holy Days were days of rest. Peasants could be fined if they were found working in the field and women were forbidden to spin thread on a Sunday.

Pilgrimages

People went to church and many went on pilgrimages as penance for sins, to ask for favours or in thanksgiving. Some of the favourite places to go on pilgrimage were Lough Derg and Croagh Patrick in Ireland or Canterbury in England.

Source D

A medieval picture of pilgrims visiting Canterbury, where Thomas Becket was murdered.

- *Why do you think people would go on pilgrimages? Do people still go on pilgrimages today? If so, where do they go?*

Monks and monasteries

The Normans also built many monasteries. These were places of learning where manuscripts were carefully written by hand, the poor were cared for, and schools and hospitals established. Kings and nobles donated money and land to the monasteries in the hope that this would save their souls.

Source E

A monk writing, taken from the Eadwine Psalter, about 1150. A great deal of the evidence about life in Norman times and the medieval period comes from the writing and drawings of the monks.

The rules of the monastery

Monks and nuns were supposed to follow strict rules which had been laid down by Saint Benedict. Monks wore long habits and had the top of their heads shaved. This hairstyle was called a tonsure and reminded monks of Jesus's crown of thorns.

A monk had to take three vows:

- poverty – he must not have possessions;
- chastity – he must not marry;
- obedience – he must obey the abbot.

Summer Timetable

Midnight	'Matins'–the first prayers of the day (for an hour)
6 am	'Prime'–prayers at sunrise (for half an hour)
	Breakfast
	Work or read
9 am	Mass (for an hour)
10 am	Meeting of all the monks in the Chapter House
11 am	Mass (for an hour)
Noon	Dinner
	Rest
2 pm	'Nones'–prayers (for half an hour)
	Work
4 pm	'Vespers'–prayers (for half an hour)
	Work
6 pm	Supper
7 pm	'Compline'–the last prayers of the day (for half an hour)
	Bed (later in summer than in winter)

- Use this timetable to answer these questions:
  a How many times did the monks pray during the day?
  b How many meals did they eat?
  c What kinds of work might the monks have done?

Source F

Consider how hard life is in a monastery. We are the soldiers of Christ fighting bravely against the devil. It is impossible to describe all the prayers, hymns and masses we say each day. Our clothes are plain, we have little food and we cannot do as we please.

Orderic Vitalis, an English monk who lived in a French monastery in the twelfth century

Bad habits

Monasteries were meant to be places of simple living and they did a great deal of good work, especially with the poorest people, but many monasteries eventually became extremely wealthy. Some of the monasteries did not keep to their strict rules and there was a great deal of criticism of monks who indulged themselves and neglected their duties.

Source G

A meal served to monks at Canterbury:

> And as to the dishes and the number thereof what shall I say? Sixteen very costly dishes or even more were placed on the table. Many kinds of fish, roast and boiled, stuffed and fried, many dishes made with eggs and pepper by skilful cooks.

> Gerald of Wales, a monk writing in the twelfth century

Priests

By the thirteenth century there were about 40,000 ordained priests in England. However, some of these priests, and even bishops, lived openly with their wives and children. Many church clergy were little better educated than the poor people that they served.

Source H

Sins of the flesh. This picture of a priest and a nun in the stocks appears to illustrate that many members of religious orders ignored their vows of chastity and behaved in a way which brought the Church into disrepute.

Friars

The first friars thought that the monasteries had grown too rich. Unlike monks they did not live in monasteries but went around the countryside preaching, hearing confession, visiting the sick and caring for the poor. These men were meant to live very humble lives, having no possessions, relying on the charity of the people they visited. By the thirteenth century, however, their rules also seemed to be less strict and they, like other religious orders, had become much less popular.

Source I

Geoffrey Chaucer described the friar in the *Canterbury Tales* as being willing to forgive people's sins in exchange for money. This is a modern translation of what Chaucer wrote:

> He knew the tavern well in every town
>
> And every innkeeper and barmaid too
>
> Better than the lepers, beggars and that crew,
>
> For in so eminent a man as he
>
> It was not fitting with the dignity
>
> Of his position dealing with the scum
>
> Of wretched lepers nothing good can come
>
> Of commerce with such slum-and-gutter dwellers,
>
> But only with the rich and victual sellers.

● *With a partner, work out what Chaucer was saying about the friar. In what ways did he seem to be breaking his vows?*

The Crusades

The Crusades were holy wars fought by the Christians against people of different religions. In the Middle Ages, people in England, and in all of western Europe, were Christians who belonged to the Catholic Church. Their religious leader was the Pope, in Rome. Parts of eastern Europe were Christian but not Catholic. They belonged to the Eastern Orthodox Church which was based in Constantinople, now called Istanbul. Beyond these areas were Islamic countries. Both Islam and Christianity regarded Jerusalem as a holy city, which they both wanted to occupy and control. This conflict led to the seven Crusades which were fought between 1099 and 1248.

In the Middle Ages life was violent and people only trusted their families and their feudal lord. The Church encouraged pilgrimages to holy places to make people live less violently. The greatest pilgrimage was to Jerusalem, where Christ had lived. People in the Middle Ages were terrified of hell. Through the suffering they endured on their journey, pilgrims hoped to make up for the sins they had committed and make sure that they got into heaven. However, law and order had broken down in Palestine and no one was safe from attack. By controlling Jerusalem, Church leaders hoped to make it safe for pilgrims to visit. Jerusalem fell to the crusaders in 1099 and was lost to Saladin's Muslim army in 1187. Although the Crusades continued for hundreds of years, during which time thousands of people were slaughtered and much destruction was caused, the Christians never regained Jerusalem.

Source J

Many different types of people became crusaders as is shown by the records of a ship which sailed from France to the East in 1250. It carried 453 crusaders, who included:

14 knights;

90 servants of the knights;

7 ministers of the Church;

300 male commoners;

42 female commoners.

Source K

Although religion was the most usual motive for crusading, Abba Eban, a modern historian, suggests that some crusaders had different reasons:

To the knights, it was a chance for adventure, looting and conquest. To the merchants of Italy, it meant reopening the trade routes in the East that had been blocked by the Muslims.

Source L

This illustration from a thirteenth-century manuscript shows some different types of Christians who went on crusades.

● *Which three types of people are shown in the picture? What different motives might they have had for going on crusade?*

Thomas Becket

In 1162, Henry II made Thomas Becket the Archbishop of Canterbury – the most important position in the English Church. For a hundred years, popes, archbishops and kings had argued about who was in charge of the Church. Henry II wanted Becket to help him to regain control of the Church and all its wealth. Thomas Becket surprised the king by refusing. Their argument became so bad that Becket had to leave the country for six years. When he returned he excommunicated all the bishops who had helped the king. This made Henry furious and he called out for someone to help him deal with Becket. Four of his knights killed the archbishop in Canterbury Cathedral in 1170.

Source M

The murder of Becket, from a thirteenth-century book of psalms, the other priest is the writer of the eye-witness account.

Source N

This is part of an eye-witness account from a monk who was with Becket when he was killed.

In a mad rage, one knight shouted, 'Where is Thomas Becket, traitor to the king and the country?' Thomas answered 'Here I am. I am no traitor to the king but a priest of God. What do you want from me?' 'Forgive those you have condemned', a knight said. 'I will not', replied the archbishop. 'Then you shall die now and get what you deserve.' 'I am ready to die for my Lord God, that through my blood the Church shall win peace and freedom.'

- *Who were the people Becket had condemned?*
- *Is there any evidence in the source that Becket wanted to be killed? What might have been gained by this?*

---

1 Giving as many examples as you can from the sources, explain why the Church played a very important part in people's lives in the Middle Ages.

2 Work in pairs. One of each pair should make a list of all the good aspects of religious life in the Middle Ages. The other should make a list of all the criticisms which could be made of religious people in those times. Explain your examples and arguments to each other.

3 Copy the table headings below and complete the table using any evidence you have found.

The Church was good	Some religious people were not good

4 How did Norman kings and the Catholic Church try to use each other's power to control the people? What does the murder of Becket tell you about the king's relationship with the Church?

The Normans in Ireland

1 Ireland before the Normans

The Normans came to Ireland in 1169. The people of Ireland spoke a form of the Celtic language, known as Gaelic. Most people lived on the land and cattle were the most important part of the economy. The country was divided into small kingdoms and the kings were often at war with their rivals. The most powerful king was known as the Ard Rí or High King.

Henry, King of England, Duke of Normandy and Aquitaine and Count of Anjou, to all his liegemen, English, Normans, Welsh and Scots sends greetings. Whensoever these our letters shall come to you, know you that we have taken Dermot, Prince of Leinster, into the bosom of our grace and good will. Whosoever shall be willing to lend aid to him in the recovery of his lands, let him know that he has our favour and permission.

2 Dermot MacMurrough and the Normans

Dermot MacMurrough, King of Leinster, had a long-running quarrel with the High King, Rory O'Connor. After being driven from his kingdom in 1166, Dermot went to ask for the help of the Normans. He visited the Norman king, Henry II, who gave him permission to bring Norman soldiers to Ireland to help win back his lands. Dermot also went to Wales, where he promised the Normans land in return for their help in battle.

3 Richard de Clare – Strongbow

The most powerful of the Norman knights to come to Ireland was Richard de Clare, whose name was Strongbow. Dermot had promised Strongbow that he could marry his daughter, Aoife, and that he would become king of Leinster when Dermot died. The English king, Henry II, became concerned that Strongbow was becoming too powerful and he travelled over to Ireland with an army to make sure that Strongbow remained loyal to him. Strongbow died in Dublin in 1176.

4 Normans versus the Irish

The Normans in Ireland were outnumbered by the native Irish but they managed to defeat them in battle and conquer nearly three-quarters of the country by 1250. The Normans' use of skilled footsoldiers, archers and knights on horseback proved to be too powerful for the Irish. Because of their poor weapons and lack of body armour, the Irish tried to avoid pitched battles with the Normans. They preferred to launch ambushes and surprise attacks in the bogs and woods.

5 John de Courcy, conqueror of Ulster

In 1177, a Norman knight named John de Courcy, who felt that he had not been rewarded for his fighting skills by the king, set out to conquer Ulster and make himself rich and powerful. He invaded the province of Ulster and defeated the Irish at a battle in Down. He built castles at Greencastle, Dundrum and Carrickfergus. The king had not given permission for de Courcy's invasion and sent an army to take him prisoner. He then made another knight, Hugh de Lacy, Earl of Ulster.

6 What became of the Normans in Ireland?

The Norman colony in Ireland declined during the thirteenth and fourteenth centuries for a number of reasons. Many Normans adopted the lifestyle and laws of the Irish. During this period, the number of Normans living in Ireland was also reduced by warfare, famine, sickness and the rise of the Gaelic lords. They left behind them a rich legacy in Ireland which includes towns, castles, churches and monasteries, place names and family names.

13

Ireland before the Normans

The first Normans arrived in Ireland in 1169, over a century after the Norman invasion of England. As a result of this long time gap, the term 'Norman' no longer accurately describes these soldiers and their followers; 'Anglo-Norman' is a better description. The Anglo-Normans were never able to gain control over Ireland in the same way as they gained control over England.

What was Ireland like before the Normans arrived in the twelfth century?

Most Irish people were descended from the Celts, the Vikings and a number of other peoples who had settled in Ireland. The Celts had come to Ireland about 300 BC. The Vikings had raided the coast of Ireland in the eighth and ninth centuries. After about AD 850 they had begun to settle and build towns in ports along the coast. The Vikings were traders and developed Irish trade along the coast and with other countries. Dublin became the centre of this trade and also the most important Viking town. As the map shows, the Vikings only ever ruled part of Ireland.

This map shows the Viking settlements in Ireland.

The Irish economy

Many Irish people were cattle farmers; dairy cows were the most important stock and supplied butter, which was vital as a food during winter. Other farmers grew grain crops and some grew flax which they made into linen. Sheep and pigs were reared for meat. Sheep's wool was mostly used for making clothes. Many Irish people who lived near to the coast were also good sailors and they made special boats known as 'currachs' from animal skin. These boats could travel great distances even in bad weather.

The Church in Ireland

Many Irish monks lived in simple walled communities centred around a small stone church. The Irish kings gave the church both protection and money. Even before the coming of the Normans, Ireland had strong links with the rest of Europe. This was mainly due to the important role played by the Irish Church in sending monks and scholars to other monasteries throughout Europe. The Irish Church also had strong links with the Church in England and with the Pope in Rome. Both the Pope and the Archbishop of Canterbury wanted to increase their influence over the Church in Ireland, but the Irish Church leaders resisted this.

Irish kings and kingdoms

Ireland was divided into a number of kingdoms each ruled by a powerful leader. The kings were often at war with each other. The Ard Rí, or High King was the most powerful Irish king and other kings had to recognise him as their overlord. This meant that they had to give him grain and cattle each year, and to give him support in his battles against his enemies. The High King in 1166 was Rory O'Connor, the King of Connacht. Dermot MacMurrough, the King of Leinster, also wanted to be High King and challenged O'Connor. This conflict between the Irish kings was to play an important part in the coming of the Normans to Ireland.

1 Write or draw three examples to show how Irish people made their living.

2 In what ways did Ireland have links with Europe before the coming of the Normans?

3 Draw a map of Ireland and mark on it the five main kingdoms.

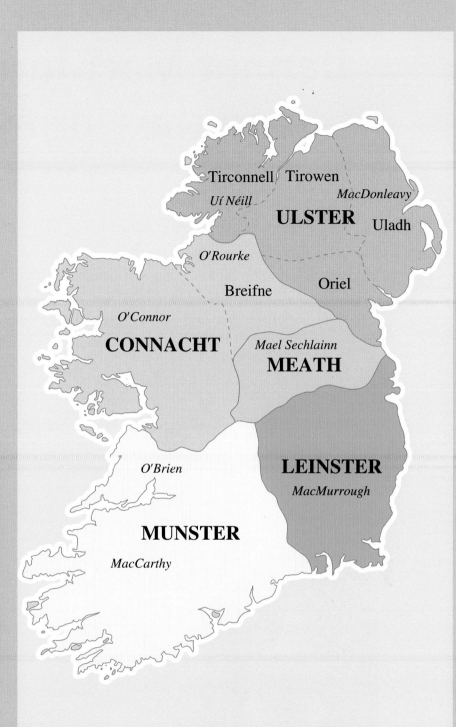

This map shows the kingdoms and sub-kingdoms in Ireland before the coming of the Normans. It also shows the names of the powerful families which controlled each region.

14

Dermot MacMurrough and the Normans

Dermot MacMurrough was king of part of Leinster. He had opposed Rory O'Connor in his bid to become High King of Ireland. When Rory did become High King in 1166, he forced Dermot out of Leinster and Dermot turned to the Normans for help.

Why did the Normans go to Ireland?

Dermot MacMurrough decided to ask Henry II, King of England, for help against O'Connor. Dermot went to visit Henry in France, taking with him a large group of followers and a store of gold. The Norman chroniclers were impressed and described him as 'the rich king of the plenteous Leinster'.

Source A

Henry II, Angevin emperor, the most powerful ruler in Western Europe.

King Henry II was born in Normandy, brought up in France, and spoke Norman French. In many ways he was more French than English. England was only one of Henry's possessions. He also had lands in France and held claims over Toulouse, Wales and Scotland. These lands were known as the Angevin Empire.

Henry had had an interest in Ireland since 1155 when the Pope, Adrian IV, had given him permission to go there. The Pope did this because he believed that the Irish Church was becoming too independent and he wanted more control over it. However, because Henry was busy with other parts of his empire, he had decided to postpone any expedition to Ireland. MacMurrough now looked like a useful ally, especially if Henry eventually decided to invade Ireland.

Source B

When MacMurrough visited Henry in France in 1166, he swore the following oath of loyalty to him. If he accepted Henry as his lord, Henry would, in turn, protect him from his enemies.

> In the presence of the barons of your empire
> Your man I shall become
> Henceforth all the days of my life
> On condition that you be my helper
> So that I do not lose everything.
> You I shall acknowledge as Sire and Lord
> In the presence of your Barons and Lords.

'The Song of Dermot and the Earl'

Source C

Although Henry promised to help MacMurrough, he was too busy with his own territories to go to Ireland himself. Instead he wrote letters asking his subjects to give support to MacMurrough.

> Know you that we have taken Dermot. Prince of Leinster, into the bosom of our grace and goodwill. Whosoever shall be willing to lend him aid in the recovery of his lands, let him know that he has our favour and permission.

This map shows the lands ruled over by Henry II. This area is known as the Angevin Empire. By the end of his life Henry II also ruled over much of eastern and southern Ireland.

Dermot MacMurrough returned to England and Wales with these letters from the king. Many of the Normans he approached for help did not possess land of their own. Dermot offered them money and land and was promised help by Norman lords and soldiers who lived on the Welsh borders and some Flemish soldiers who had settled in Wales 60 years earlier.

MacMurrough's most powerful ally was Richard FitzGilbert de Clare, better known as Strongbow. MacMurrough promised Strongbow that, in exchange for his help, he could marry MacMurrough's daughter, Aoife, and that he would inherit the kingdom of Leinster when MacMurrough died.

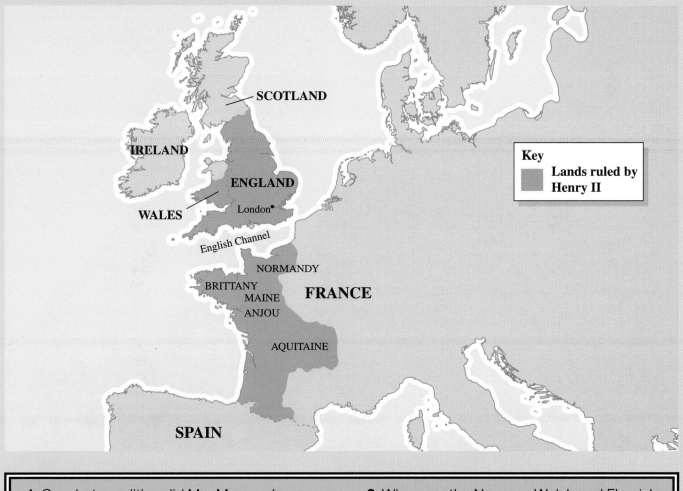

Key
Lands ruled by Henry II

---

1 On what condition did MacMurrough agree to give his loyalty to Henry?

2 Why was Henry willing to support MacMurrough?

3 Why were the Norman, Welsh and Flemish soldiers willing to support MacMurrough?

4 Why do you think MacMurrough promised his daughter to Strongbow?

The Normans come to Ireland

The first large group of Normans, probably about 600 soldiers, including knights on horses, archers and foot soldiers, came to Ireland in 1169. They were well-equipped and well-protected. They were armed with long lances and wore helmets and coats of mail and carried shields. Many of the Irish warriors were lightly clad and armed with only axes, slings or javelins. MacMurrough and a few hundred of his followers joined the Normans and marched to Wexford town, which they quickly captured. This swift victory alarmed the Irish kings, who agreed to recognise MacMurrough as king of Leinster, south of Dublin, if he promised to get rid of his foreign allies and accept O'Connor as High King of Ireland. MacMurrough did not keep this promise; more Normans arrived in Ireland, taking land in Wexford and Waterford. In August 1170, Strongbow, a Welsh Norman, arrived in Ireland and completed the taking of Waterford.

Source D

The Normans land in Ireland, a drawing by Alphonse de Neuville, 1870.

● *Does the Norman army look like a strong one?*

Source E

This description of Strongbow was written by Gerald of Wales:

> He had reddish hair and freckles, grey eyes and a feminine face, a weak voice and a short neck, though in almost all other respects he was of tall build. He was a generous and easy going man. What he could not accomplish by deed he settled by persuasiveness of his words. When he took up his position in the midst of battle, he stood firm as an immovable standard around which his men could regroup and take refuge. In war he remained steadfast and reliable, in good fortune and bad alike.

Source F

This was written by a modern historian in 1987:

> As a member of the powerful de Clare family, with its lands and supporters in Normandy and England, Wales, and now Ireland, Strongbow could not be lightly dismissed or suppressed. He was brave in battle, but shrewd and no hot-head.

F.X. Martin, *A New History of Ireland*.

● *How do these two descriptions agree?*

Source G

The wedding of Strongbow and Aoife. Following the capture of Waterford, MacMurrough kept his promise and let Strongbow marry his daughter, Aoife. This picture of their wedding was painted in the nineteenth century. It suggests that the marriage of Aoife and Strongbow took place as soon as the battle was over, in the midst of the dead and dying. This was not true but the picture correctly suggests that the marriage was regarded as part of the Norman victory.

● *Describe the scene in the wedding painting.*

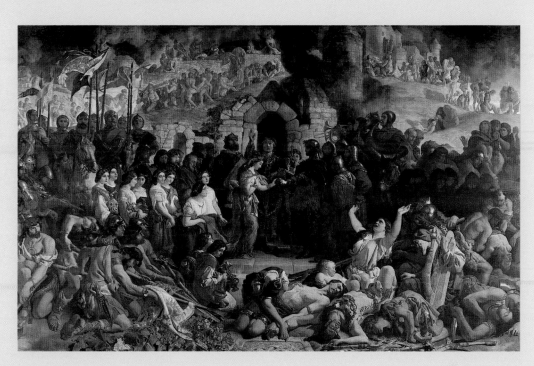

The capture of Dublin

After MacMurrough and the Normans had control of the old Viking cities of Wexford and Waterford, they set off to capture Dublin from Rory O'Connor and his allies. The Normans arrived in Dublin before O'Connor's army and they took the city and burned it. O'Connor did try to recapture Dublin but the Normans, who knew they were greatly outnumbered, made a surprise attack on the Irish soldiers in their camp and defeated them. MacMurrough died shortly afterwards, in May 1171. Strongbow was declared the new king of Leinster, which included the important ports of Dublin, Wexford and Waterford. Within the space of just a few years, a Norman had become the king of the most important kingdom in Ireland.

---

1 Make a timeline. Include the following events:
● MacMurrough dies;
● MacMurrough returns to Ireland after securing a promise of help from the Normans;
● Strongbow lands near Waterford;
● MacMurrough goes to seek help from Henry II;
● Rory O'Connor drives MacMurrough out of the kingdom of Leinster;
● Aoife marries Strongbow.

2 Explain the reasons why the Normans came to Ireland.

3 Write a short report explaining whether or not events turned out the way MacMurrough had hoped. You could make lists of his gains and losses. Overall, which do you think is the greater?

4 Write a play showing what Aoife's attitude might have been to her marriage.

15

Strongbow and Henry II

Strongbow was a powerful Norman lord and an experienced war leader. However, when MacMurrough approached him, he had lost some of his land and was out of favour with Henry II. In return for supporting MacMurrough, he was promised land in Ireland and the right to inherit the kingdom of Leinster. Within a few years he had achieved all of this.

How did Henry react to Strongbow's growing power in Ireland?

When Dermot MacMurrough died in 1171, Strongbow became King of Leinster. Not everyone was happy with this arrangement. The Leinster Vikings revolted and attacked Dublin. After some fierce fighting, they were defeated by the Normans. The Irish kings were afraid that they would lose their power to the Normans. They banded together and tried to recapture Dublin but they also failed.

Henry visits Ireland

Another response to Strongbow's kingship came, not from the Vikings or the Irish, but from Henry II. Although he had been happy for Strongbow and the other Normans to undertake a risky adventure in Ireland, he was alarmed when they were successful. Henry was determined that he should be the only Norman ruler in Ireland.

Strongbow knew that he had angered Henry by declaring himself to be a king, and he decided to travel to England to make peace with Henry, to pay homage to him and give him some of the lands in Leinster. Although Henry accepted Strongbow's loyalty and gifts, he felt that it was important to visit Ireland personally. Henry arrived in Waterford in October 1171. He brought with him 400 ships, 500 knights and 4,000 archers and foot soldiers. His journey through Ireland was a triumph, and the Normans, the Irish and the Vikings all paid homage to him. In return, Strongbow was allowed to be a lord, not a king. Another Norman knight, Hugh de Lacy, was appointed as Henry's representative in Ireland. The main reason for this appears to have been to hold Strongbow in check.

The Irish kings were glad of Henry's protection against Strongbow, and many of them swore loyalty to Henry. They also signed a treaty with him in 1175 which divided Ireland into Norman and Irish areas. Rory O'Connor pledged to recognise Henry as overlord and, in return, Henry agreed to accept O'Connor as High King. He would be the last High King in Ireland.

Henry and the Irish Church

Henry had been given the permission of the Pope, Adrian IV, to invade Ireland. Adrian wanted to bring the Irish Church more under the influence of Rome. However, in 1171, the new Pope, Alexander III, was angry with Henry because of the murder of Thomas Becket, the Archbishop of Canterbury. Henry thought that a visit to Ireland would allow him to win back the support of the Pope. In 1172 Henry met the Irish bishops and other members of the Irish Church in Cashel. As a result, the Irish Church agreed to recognise the Pope's authority.

Ireland after Henry

When Henry left Ireland, he had subdued both the Irish kings and the Norman lords, and he had made peace with the Pope. But the promises which were made, both during and after Henry's visit, were never kept. The Norman lords and barons continued to seize more land, and even Henry gave grants of Irish land when it suited him. Although O'Connor continued to be High King in name, he had little real authority.

The Normans come to Ireland

1166 Rory O'Connor becomes High King of Ireland. His enemy and rival, Dermot MacMurrough, asks Henry II, King of England, for help. Henry agrees. MacMurrough also asks Welsh knights for support.

1169 Welsh knights and soldiers land in Ireland and capture Wexford.

1170 Strongbow, another Welsh Norman knight, lands in Waterford, which he and MacMurrough capture. MacMurrough becomes King of Leinster. Strongbow marries Aoife, MacMurrough's daughter, and becomes the heir to the kingdom of Leinster.

1171 MacMurrough dies; Strongbow becomes King of Leinster. Henry II lands in Waterford with many knights and soldiers. He receives homage from Strongbow and all the lords.

1172 Henry is recognised as Lord of Ireland by all Norman and most Irish kings and lords.

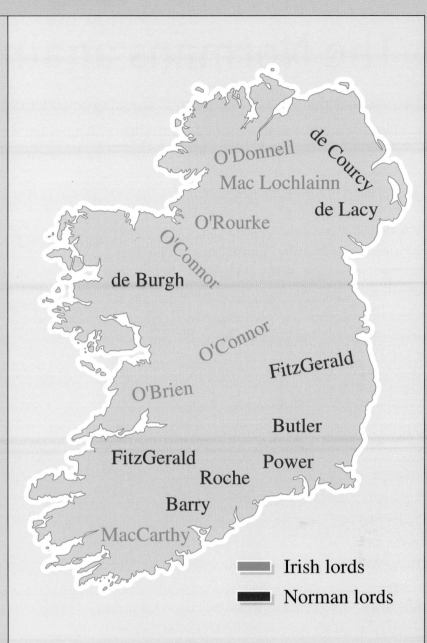

Irish lords

Norman lords

This map shows how the Norman lords conquered many areas of Ireland. However, they did not take control of the whole country.

- *Which areas were still controlled by Irish lords?*

1 Write an account of Strongbow's life under the following headings:
- why Strongbow came to Ireland;
- Strongbow's achievements in Ireland;
- Strongbow's dealings with Henry II.

2 How did the Pope and the Church influence Henry's attitude to Ireland?

3 Why did the Irish kings welcome Henry to Ireland?

16

The Normans against the Irish

By 1250, less than 100 years after their arrival in Ireland, three-quarters of Ireland had been taken over by the Normans. The Irish were known to be brave warriors and they outnumbered the Normans. The Normans also had little support from their kings.

Why were the Normans able to defeat the Irish and take so much of their land?

When the Normans came to Ireland, they were already experienced fighters. They brought the skills that they had learnt in England, Wales and France to Ireland. This gave them a great advantage over their enemies.

Source A

In warfare, the Normans owed much to their technical skills and discipline as fighting men. Their use of cavalry, with mounted knights working as a unit, gave them an advantage over all the opponents they encountered in Britain. In the eleventh and early twelfth centuries, the knight was not a man of high social standing; he was a trained fighter with expensive equipment.

David Walker, *The Normans in Britain,* 1995

The Irish warriors soon learnt to avoid direct battles with the Normans on open land, but tried to ambush them in the bogs and forests where they could use slings to hurl stones at the Norman soldiers. Despite this, the Irish were still no match for knights who were protected from head to foot by mail armour and shields.

Source B
The simpleness of the Irish weapons was observed at the time.

They regard weapons as a burden and think it honourable to fight unarmed. They use three types of weapons – short spears, darts, and big axes.

Gerald of Wales

Source C
The Normans were famous for their strategic skill in planning their battles and their use of superior weapons.

The Normans who came to Ireland were seasoned fighters against the Welsh, whose tactics and weapons were much the same as the Irish. The Normans advanced into battle on an organised plan, unlike the Irish who charged in disarray. The Normans were superior in their weapons – the long sword, the lance, the iron helmet, the hauberk of mail covering body, thighs and arms – contrasting with the Irish soldier carrying his axe and short sword, and clad in a linen tunic. One of the most feared groups of the invaders were the Welsh archers with their long bows; the Irish spear, javelin, and sling-stones, hitherto so effective, were no match for the far-flying arrows of the Welsh.

F. X. Martin, *The Normans: Arrival and Settlement,* 1984

1 Make a list of the weapons used in battle by:
● the Irish;
● the Normans.

2 On the battlefield, who do you think had a better chance of winning and why?

A modern illustration of a battle between a Norman knight and Irish soldiers.

● *Look at how the soldiers are equipped. Who do you think would win and why?*

17

John de Courcy

The most powerful Norman lords in Ireland built castles, both for homes and for protection. One of the most successful of these was John de Courcy, who ruled Ulster for 27 years. De Courcy was finally defeated, not by the Irish, but by a Norman army who feared he was setting himself up as a king.

Who was John de Courcy and what was his impact on Ireland?

In 1177 John de Courcy, a knight from Somerset, collected about 300 troops from Dublin and marched north to the kingdom of Uladh (Down and Antrim). De Courcy was known to be daring and a fierce fighter.

Source A

A man of courage and a born fighter, always in the front line and always taking upon himself the greatest amount of danger.

Gerald of Wales

Although de Courcy and other Norman knights in Dublin had fought bravely for Henry II, they had received no reward. They wanted to conquer other parts of Ireland and become rich and powerful. De Courcy and his followers invaded Ulster and captured the capital, Down. Although the Irish kings gathered an army to challenge de Courcy, they were defeated. Apart from being a great soldier, de Courcy was also very cunning and used the superstitious and religious beliefs of the Irish people to his own advantage. The city of Down was renamed Downpatrick, after St Patrick, and de Courcy also showed how his conquest of Ulster appeared to fit in with two prophecies. One, attributed to St Columba, said that Downpatrick would be captured by a stranger with a small army.

Source B

The second prophecy was quoted by Gerald of Wales as a prophecy of Merlin:

A white knight, astride a white horse, bearing a device of birds on his shield will be the first to enter Ulidia and overrun it with hostile intent.

Source C

A modern illustration of John de Courcy.

De Courcy in Ulster

In order to keep control of his new lands, de Courcy built many castles. Towns often developed around these castles such as those at Downpatrick, Dromore, Newry, Dundrum, Carlingford, Carrickfergus and Coleraine. Abbeys or religious houses were also built. These religious communities helped to strengthen de Courcy's control over Ulster. In 1180, de Courcy married Affreca, the daughter of King Gottred of the Isle of Man. This strengthened his position in Ulster as it gave him a close ally who owned ships, which could keep de Courcy's coastal castles supplied with goods and protected from enemies.

Source E

The remains of Grey Abbey, County Down a Cistercian abbey founded by Affreca, John de Courcy's wife.

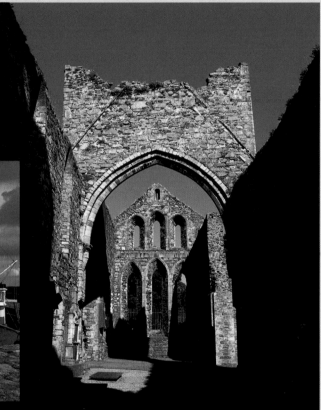

Source D

Carrickfergus Castle built by John de Courcy.

De Courcy's downfall

De Courcy had never been given permission from the king to create a lordship in Ulster. Both Henry II and Richard I allowed de Courcy to remain in Ulster, but King John, who came to the throne in 1199, was jealous of de Courcy. For many years, de Courcy had been striking his own coins in his own name, using the title Prince of Ulidia. King John used this as an excuse to move against him. He gave Hugh de Lacy, son of the Lord of Meath, permission to invade Ulster. Following this, King John made de Lacy Earl of Ulster and gave him the lands held by de Courcy. De Courcy was imprisoned briefly and, after he was set free, he lived abroad in relative poverty and obscurity.

1 Design a shield for de Courcy which shows the important stages in his life.

2 What type of warrior was de Courcy? Sources A–C might help you.

3 Research a list of castles, settlements and monasteries founded in Ulster.

4 What does de Courcy's rise and fall from power show you about the role of the king?

5 Write a death notice for de Courcy either praising or criticising his achievements.

18

What became of the Normans?

By the thirteenth century, the Normans controlled much of Ireland, but by the fifteenth century they controlled only a small area known as the Pale, around Dublin.

What were the reasons for this decline and how did they affect the Normans in Ireland?

If we look for reasons which cause a population or a colony of strangers to decrease we might come up with a list like this:

Change of ways
The strangers become more and more like the native people.

War
Large numbers of people die in war. Strangers lose their land.

Famine
Many people starve to death, others leave their homes.

Disease
An epidemic causes sickness and death for a large number of people.

After 1300 the Norman or English colony in Ireland decreased because of all these reasons. To find out what happened let us look at each reason in turn and find out how it affected Ireland.

Change of ways
By the fourteenth century many Norman lords had become Gaelicised. That means they became more like the Irish.

Source A
Royal decree from the king of England in 1360:

> Many of the English nation have again become like Irishmen and send their children among the Irish to be nursed and taught the Irish tongue, so that people of the English race have become Irish.

War
Many English lords were also defeated by Irish chieftains who fought to regain their lands. Although the English had always been better-equipped soldiers, the Irish now also began to wear armour and hired Scottish soldiers called 'gallowglasses'. They were professional soldiers descended from fierce Viking warriors and, with their armour, shields, huge swords and axes, they were a match for any Norman knight in battle.

Source B

A gallowglass, carved in stone at Glinsk, County Galway. 'Gallowglass' means foreign warrior. These heavily-armed professional soldiers first came to Ireland from Scotland in the late thirteenth century. They hired themselves out to Irish kings and lords and, by the late fifteenth century, their descendents were working in all parts of the country, for chiefs and lords alike, as bodyguards, police or as elite troops in the army.

The Bruce invasions

In 1314 the Scottish king, Robert Bruce, had defeated the English at the Battle of Bannockburn. The Irish lords believed that Bruce could help them to defeat the English colony in Ireland and, in 1315, Bruce sent his brother, Edward, to Ireland with an army of 6,000 men. Edward was joined by many Irish and began to capture land and castles from the English, including Carrickfergus. In 1316 Edward Bruce was crowned king of Ireland and in 1317 he and his brother Robert attempted to conquer more English lands in Ireland. This reinforced Scottish army pillaged and plundered everything in its path and left a trail of destroyed farms, villages, English manors and towns. The Scots failed to capture the city of Dublin and in 1318 Edward Bruce was finally defeated and killed at the battle of Faughart, near Dundalk where he had earlier been crowned king. As a result of the invasion, the English colony in Ireland was severely reduced but the warfare had been so savage and destructive that the Irish were also glad to see it end.

Source D

A statue of Robert Bruce, the Scottish king, at Bannockburn, the site of his great victory over the armies of the English king, Edward II.

Source C

At Carrickfergus the English garrison seized 30 Scots as hostages. A Dublin writer reported that eight of the hostages were later eaten by the starving garrison which was reduced to cannibalism. Carrickfergus finally surrendered to the Scots in September 1316.

Colm McNamee, 'The Bruce Invasions of Ireland', in *History Ireland,* Spring 1993

Famine

As war raged in Ireland a terrible famine, due to the poor harvests between 1315 and 1318, added to the disasters of the English colony. Crops failed and cattle died from disease, leaving a shortage of food especially in the English farming areas. The rampaging Bruce armies also burned farms and destroyed crops, worsening the effects of the famine. English farms, manors and villages were destroyed and the numbers of the English fell rapidly.

Disease – the Black Death

In the Middle Ages many people died from a whole range of diseases including influenza, measles and smallpox. They did not know that germs caused disease and so had few real treatments or cures. The worst epidemic was the Black Death in the 1300s. It was so widespread and horrible that many believed it was the end of the world.

Source E

This description of the effects of the Black Death on towns and villages was written in 1395:

Many villages and hamlets became deserted. Sheep and cattle went wandering over fields and through crops and there was no one to look after them.

The illness began with tiredness and a high temperature followed by the appearance of small boils on the body. These boils or buboes grew larger and turned black, giving the plague its common name – the Black Death. Small red spots next appeared on the stomach and were quickly followed by internal bleeding and death. Anyone touching the victim could become infected.

Source F

Father Clyn, who wrote this description of the Black Death, was a Franciscan Friar who recorded events in Kilkenny. He also seems to have died from this plague in about 1349.

This disease is so contagious that those who touched the dead or persons sick with the plague were at once infected and died. Many died from boils and ulcers and running sores which grew on the legs and beneath the armpits, others suffered pains in the head and went into a frenzy, whilst others spat blood.

● *How did the disease get its name?*
● *How reliable is Father Clyn's description as evidence of the plague?*
● *In which country did the Black Death begin ?*

This map shows the route of the Black Death in 1348–9. It came from the east and was carried to Europe by traders. It spread rapidly, destroying whole communities with great speed.

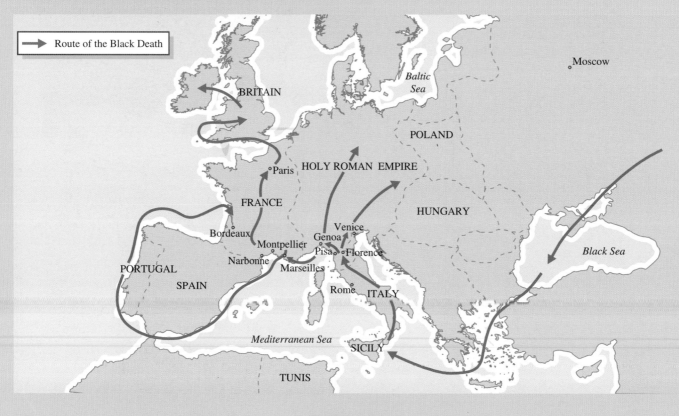

Source G

A reconstruction of a scene from the Black Death in the Dublinia Exhibition in Dublin.
● *Make a list of the different causes of the Black Death according to people at the time.*

Causes and treatment of the disease

The most likely explanation for the Black Death is that it was a mixture of bubonic plague and other illnesses such as pneumonia. Bubonic plague is spread from infected fleas carried by rats. The fleas land on humans and thus spread the disease. Living conditions in towns and cities in the Middle Ages were so filthy and overcrowded that the disease very quickly took hold. Doctors could do little to treat the victims except lance the boils to drain off the horrible-smelling black liquid or bathe the patient in vinegar.

Priests claimed that the plague was a punishment from God for peasants who did not respect the Church. Some people were so afraid that they beat themselves in public to make up for their sins in the hope that this would protect them from the plague.

Some figures say that almost half the population of Britain died during the Black Death. In Ireland, the towns, manors and villages of the English suffered most and took centuries to recover. Many English fled back to England, leaving their homes deserted. Farms were abandoned and grew wild. One archbishop claimed that two-thirds of the English population in Ireland were killed by the Black Death.

1 Plan a short essay explaining the reasons for the decline of the Normans in Ireland.
● Choose a suitable title.
● Make a list of the reasons.
● For each reason write notes to explain how it affected the Normans.
● Select phrases or sentences from the sources which will show evidence for your explanations.
● Decide on a summary of points to end your essay.
● Write the essay in your own words. Break it into paragraphs each with a heading.

The Norman legacy

The Normans and their successors have left a long and enduring legacy in all the countries in which they settled including England, Wales, Scotland and Ireland. Some aspects of the Norman legacy are easy to see, especially Norman buildings such as castles and churches. Other aspects are not so obvious, for example the changes the Normans made to the organisation of the Church and the government.

Castles

Castles were important to the Normans, both to live in and as a means of defending themselves. They were also a sign to the local population that the Normans intended to stay for a long time. In Ireland alone, almost 2,000 castles are thought to have been built by the descendants of the Normans.

Trim Castle in Co. Meath, built in the twelfth and thirteenth centuries. The castle is built by the River Boyne, and was the headquarters of the de Lacys, the lords of Meath. It was, for long, the largest castle in Ireland.

Churches

Many of the oldest surviving church buildings in these countries were built by the Normans.

The ruins of Inch Abbey in Downpatrick, Co. Down, built by John de Courcy on the site of an Irish monastery his knights had destroyed. It was the first building in Ireland in the Gothic style (with pointed arches).

Surnames

Many surnames are of Norman origin. Some examples of this are Power, Burke, Fitzwilliam, Wogan, Lynch and Fitzgerald.

Butler

The Butlers were one of the most important of the Norman-Irish families. When Theobald Fitzwalter was made Chief Butler of Ireland by Henry II in 1177, the family became known as Butler. They became the Earls of Ormond, the most important of many titles conferred on them.

Language

The Normans who first settled in England spoke French, English and Latin, although French was their everyday language. Gradually this was replaced by English. When the Normans eventually invaded Wales, Scotland and Ireland they took with them the English language.

This signpost shows place names both in Gaelic and in English. Before the Normans came to Ireland, the people of Ireland spoke Gaelic.

Towns

Except for Ulster, most of the towns in Ireland were founded by the Normans. Places such as New Ross, Kilkenny, Galway and Athlone became important centres for commerce.

Law and order

The Normans reorganised the system of central and local government. They introduced a parliament to Ireland.

This picture shows the present Irish parliament in Dublin, the Dail.

Carlingford town, Co. Louth, probably the best-preserved Norman town in Ireland. The ruins of King John's castle overlook the harbour.